AN ADVENTURE

by

C. A. E. MOBERLY

and

E. F. JOURDAIN

edited by

JOAN EVANS

Martino Fine Books
Eastford, CT
2019

Martino Fine Books
P.O. Box 913,
Eastford, CT 06242 USA

ISBN   978-1-68422-304-6

Copyright 2019
Martino Fine Books

Cover Design Tiziana Matarazzo

Printed in the United States of America On 100% Acid-Free Paper

AN ADVENTURE

by

C. A. E. MOBERLY

and

E. F. JOURDAIN

edited by

JOAN EVANS

FABER AND FABER
24 Russell Square
London

First published in mcmxi
Published in this fifth edition mcmlv
by Faber and Faber Limited
24 Russell Square London W.C.1
Printed in Great Britain by
R. MacLehose and Company Limited
The University Press Glasgow

Contents

———————•◦•◦◦))◌◊◌◊◌◔◦◔◦◔◌◊◌◊◌((◦•◦◦•———————

7

Illustrations

9

MAPS OF PETIT TRIANON (Plates II and III)

A Key gives the names of the features and the numbers refer to:

1. Cour Royale
2. Le Château
3. Le Jeu de Bague
4. La Rotonde
5. La Grotte
6. La Serre
7. Reservoir
8. Le Belvédère
9. Logement du Jardinier
10. La Comédie
11. La Laiterie
12. Pavillon
13. L'Orangerie
14. Cour des Cuisines
15. La Chapelle

Maps

SKETCH MAP ILLUSTRATING THE ROUTE TAKEN BY MISS
MOBERLY AND MISS JOURDAIN ON THE 10TH AUGUST,
1901

at the end of the book

MIQUE'S MAP OF THE GARDENS OF THE TRIANON

at the end of the book

ENLARGED SECTION OF MIQUE'S MAP

at the end of the book

VERSAILLES AND THE TRIANONS IN 1898

at the end of the book

From a plan made by Marcel Lambert

11

Editor's Preface (1955)

It is now more than fifty years since Miss Moberly and Miss Jourdain had their 'adventure' at Versailles; yet people still read the book in which they recounted it. *An Adventure* has appeared in several editions,[1] the more recent of which are not identical (except in the fundamental narratives) with the first. I have thought it well to make a fresh edition, as close as possible to that first published, though giving throughout the authors' real names and not the *noms de guerre* they felt it discreet to employ in 1911. I have excluded some later accretions,[2] and have checked the text against the original MSS.[3]

Miss Moberly was born in 1846, and died in 1937; Miss Jourdain was born in 1864 and died in 1924. The number of people who knew them both diminishes every year. As one of these, I may perhaps be permitted to attempt a brief sketch of them—a sketch deliberately unsoftened and even unflattering—that those who read their book without having known them may have some idea of what manner of women they were.

Charlotte Anne Elizabeth Moberly was the seventh child of

[1] First edition, 1911; second, with additional matter, 1913; third, with further additional matter and some omissions, 1924; fourth, with some omissions but with further additional matter, 1931. Each edition has been reprinted.

[2] The 1913 edition prints further documents; the 1931 edition has a preface by Edith Olivier and a 'Note' by J. W. Dunne.

[3] I have attempted in a few instances, by adding initials and dates of publication, to identify the books to which they refer; they were, for the most part, fairly new and well known when they wrote, but are less obvious now.

Editor's Preface

George Moberly, Bishop of Salisbury.[1] She was appointed Principal of St. Hugh's Hall, Oxford, on its foundation in 1886 and was still in command when I entered the College as an undergraduate in 1914. She was a dark, strong-featured woman with no feminine charm but a delightful old-fashioned voice. She had the narrow square head often found in the middle ranks of the Anglican clergy; she looked, indeed, far more clerical than did her father in the engraving that hung in her room. She was of too old a generation of women to have received an academic education; but since she came of a family of fifteen, seven of them boys, and since her father had been the Headmaster of Winchester before his promotion to the see of Salisbury, and since most of her brothers had distinguished academic careers, she was familiar with the standards if not with the practice of good scholarship. She was not particularly competent in practical things, but was skilled and exact in verbal usage. Her sound English was recognized, even when *An Adventure* was published pseudonymously, as that of a cultivated gentlewoman. She could read, but would not try to speak, French; knew some Italian and a little Latin and New Testament Greek and the elements of Hebrew.

Her interests were theological: she published *Five Visions of the Revelation* about 1914 and *The Faith of the Prophets*[2] in 1916. All through her long tenure of the Principalship of St. Hugh's she delivered a divinity lecture of respectable length to the students every Sunday evening in term.

Miss Moberly's father believed himself to be the grandson of an illegitimate daughter of Peter the Great;[3] her mother had been brought up in Italy and remained foreign in many of her ways; but Miss Moberly herself always seemed exceedingly English. A god-daughter of Charlotte Yonge, she had been

[1] A short study of her was published by Edith Olivier in *Four Victorian Ladies of Wiltshire*, 1945.
[2] A second edition was published in 1939.
[3] The story is discredited in A. P. Oppé, *Alexander and John Robert Cozens*, 1952, p. 2.

1. CHARLOTTE ANNE ELIZABETH MOBERLY
from a painting by W. Llewellyn, 1889
St. Hugh's College, Oxford

brought up in the characteristic mid-Victorian lady's culture of her circle: John Keble's *Christian Year*, de la Motte Fouqué's *Sintram*, a little Dante, and the novels of Miss Ferrier.

In spite of her membership of a large family Miss Moberly was in general society painfully shy. She lacked the breadth of interest and flexibility of mind that easy social intercourse demands; she was apt to take dislikes to people; she found little interest in the minds and temperaments of people not immediately congenial to her. She really knew very little of the world outside the Closes of Winchester and Salisbury. Her occasional flashes of insight and shrewdness were always astonishing. She was incapable of silliness, but rather looked down on acumen. Her true monument is her history of her own family—*Dulce Domum*, published in 1911—in which a restricted subject and a quasi-anonymity left her free to show her powers. No one who reads that book will dismiss her as the inexpressive woman, of narrow interests and experience, as which she might otherwise have been remembered; and no one who reads that book will underestimate the faith in which she was brought up and found her strength.

Eleanor Frances Jourdain was a woman of far greater charm, with a modest and muted elegance that grew with the years. She was short, with fine small bones, beautiful little hands, a delicately chiselled nose and very bright grey eyes. Her hair, sandy when she was a girl, early turned a silvery white and became her chief beauty.

Like Miss Moberly, Miss Jourdain was a member of a large clerical family: there were ten at Ashbourne Rectory. Her father, a man of little force but considerable charm, got no further preferment; and as he had small private means, the family tended to be centrifugal. She did not live, as Miss Moberly did, in a family circle.

Miss Jourdain went to Lady Margaret Hall as a student in 1883, and read for the Women's School of Modern History; she was awarded a second in her final Schools. A college contemporary[1] has described her as 'a curious and baffling personality, as far as I can judge a psychological egoist, absorbed in her own mental and emotional processes . . .' Miss Jourdain played an unimportant part in a rather brilliant year that included women as gifted as Gertrude Lowthian Bell, Maggie Benson and Agnes Tait. Yet she was herself gifted, if not as richly as they in wealth and position: gifted with artistic sensibility and quickness in all things, with great powers of practical improvisation, and a capacity to make a little go a long way: yet a woman of many talents rather than of one dominating gift.[2]

Miss Jourdain came of French Huguenot stock. She never set foot in France until she was thirty, when she paid a short visit to Dunkirk; she did not get as far as Paris until 1900, when she was thirty-six. France, however, became the country of her spiritual adoption; its philosophy and its drama remained her chief interests for the rest of her life. She read French easily and spoke and wrote it well, if in the slightly foreign fashion of one who has learned it in England. She had, indeed acquired it with the elements of German and Italian at a private school in Manchester at which she spent the years between fourteen and eighteen.

She was highly intelligent, and rather impatient of the niceties of pure scholarship; she had much *finesse*, though she did not mind simplicity in her subordinates; she had beautiful manners, but no gift for intimacy; she was always rather detached, and hardly ever impulsive in emotion though sometimes in judgment. Her enthusiasms were very rarely for people, and then for people she did not know; more usually her fires were lit

[1] Janet E. Courtney, *Recollected in Tranquillity*, 1926, p. 104.
[2] Her published works include a doctoral thesis written for the University of Paris, *Le symbolisme dans la Divine Comédie de Dante*, Paris, 1903 (English translation, *A Study in the Symbolism of the Divina Commedia*, Shaldon, 1902); *The Theory of the Infinite in Modern Thought*, 1911; *An Introduction to French Classical Drama*, 1912; and *Dramatic Theory and Practice in France*, 1921.

2. ELEANOR FRANCES JOURDAIN c. 1912

into admiration by artistic creation. She had a strong sense of duty to her family and her school, and later her college, and never stinted time or energy in fulfilling it; yet, except in the knowledge that such work was useful and recognised, she got little satisfaction out of it. Her religious interests lay rather in the history of mysticism than in theology; she was, however, as unquestioning and orthodox an Anglican as was Miss Moberly.

She had real artistic gifts, and was conscious that had she had time and training she might have attained distinction in water-colours. She would have wished to be a painter or a mystical philosopher: yet fate turned her first into a school-mistress and then into a woman don.

After Miss Jourdain went down from Oxford she taught in schools of various types, until about 1894, in partnership with a friend, she started a private school at Watford which I attended. A little later, I believe through her college contemporary Maggie Benson, she made the acquaintance of Miss Moberly, who had already been Principal of St. Hugh's for more than a decade. Without academic qualifications herself, Miss Moberly naturally depended on the help of a better qualified Vice-Principal. She did not find it easy to discover one who would work under her for long. Early in 1901 she thought of offering the post to Miss Jourdain. A tentative suggestion was made, and was tentatively welcomed. The visit to Paris together which resulted in their 'adventure' was arranged, partly to see how they got on together.

In fact they had the right sort of likenesses and differences for companionship. They shared an appreciation of reticence and a dislike of sentimentality; they both had an intelligent interest in the Anglican faith; they both appreciated an extremely English mid-Victorian tradition of culture, conduct and manners. The subsequent years brought them a common task in the administration of St. Hugh's and a common *parergon* in the historical documentation of *An Adventure*.

Editor's Preface

Miss Moberly had the more exact and less creative mind of the two, but could enjoy the overtones of fact. Miss Jourdain had the stronger sense of beauty and liked a little strangeness in its proportion: but the strangeness had to be of accident and the beauty of essence. As a practising amateur artist, she was perhaps the more observant of the two, but she observed impressions rather than separate facts. She had, too, a stronger appreciation of style in the things she saw, but it was a curiously unlearned appreciation. She had read a certain amount of art criticism and aesthetics, but had made no study of the history of art; indeed she distrusted such studies, feeling that they must weaken and distort aesthetic emotion.

The relation between the two women was based on age and social position. Miss Moberly was nearly twenty years older than Miss Jourdain; she was a bishop's daughter and the head of a college. Though she might be the less able and gifted woman of the two, she found it natural to regard Miss Jourdain as a kind of lady-in-waiting; and Miss Jourdain, though it might sometimes annoy her, was not unwilling to accept the position. Thus there was nothing strange in the fact that Miss Moberly should decide what researches should be made, and expect Miss Jourdain to carry them out; and that Miss Jourdain should sometimes carry them out a little reluctantly. Both had a professional life to carry on, which had to take precedence of any other work; and, at all events at first, neither took their 'adventure' very seriously. A characteristic letter from Miss Moberly to Miss Jourdain, written in November 1901[1], says: 'I am trying to write out my story of August 10th., but as I won't allow psychical doubtful incidents to take precedence of my Sunday work' (that is, the writing of a divinity lecture) 'it gets on slowly.'

Neither of them had had any training in experimental science, nor, in 1901, any experience in historical research. They were accustomed to accepting literary sources as evidence in history

[1] Bodley MS. Eng. misc. d. 249 f. 20.

18

Editor's Preface

and in religion. Neither had had any experience of experimental psychical research and they never at any time engaged in it.[1] They both always had an innate horror of any sort of spiritualism. Neither of them ever *sought* psychical experience. It is entirely characteristic that Miss Jourdain, going alone to Versailles in January 1902 after their first visit together, did not follow the same route as they had on that occasion; and that when in September 1908 she had a renewal of psychic experience near the old 'logement du corps de garde' she decided to go 'straight out by the lane'.

Many people have wondered that they did not discuss their adventure more quickly after its happening; but those who knew them both, and remember that at that time the two women were friendly but hardly intimate, would expect nothing else. Even when *An Adventure* had been published, and its authorship revealed, they only talked of their experiences to those who raised the subject with them. Many of those who saw much of them in the years after 1911 must never have heard them mention the Petit Trianon.

The story of how they came to record their experiences is told in some editions of their book. On November 25 and 28, 1901, each wrote an account for their own use, to discover what they had seen in common.[2] Then, later in November and early in December, they wrote fuller accounts for their friends. These

[1] They both refused to join the Oxford Psychical Society when it was founded in 1905. A measure of distrust and impatience can be detected in all their later correspondence with the Society for Psychical Research; they expected their word to be taken and could not take the Society's demands for records sufficiently seriously. See W. H. Salter, 'An Adventure, a Note on the Evidence,' in *Journal* of the S.P.R., Jan.–Feb. 1950, XXXV, p. 178.

[2] These accounts were printed in the 1913 ed., pp. 183 and 189. Copies of them, made in 1906, will be found in Bodley MS. Eng. misc. d. 249. They were sent to the S.P.R. in October 1902 before any research had been attempted. It was rather unfavourably reviewed in the *Proceedings of the Society for Psychical Research* in June, 1911. For a fair and interesting criticism of them see W. H. Salter, *ibid.*, Jan.–Feb. 1950, p. 178.

accounts are those printed with slight variations as the main narrative of *An Adventure*. I have checked them against the manuscript originals and have indicated the insignificant divergencies, nearly all dictated by the wish to preserve the authors' anonymity.

Long before it was published the story had been told to some of their friends.[1] Some of these friends accompanied them as witnesses on their later researches; I remember going to Versailles with my mother and Miss Jourdain in 1910 and examining the Chapel door and the possible ways out of the Jardin Français.

In 1911 Mr. Stephen Paget was entrusted with the manuscript of *An Adventure* with a view to securing its publication. He took it to Macmillan's and persuaded them to undertake it. It came out in that year, with the authors disguised under the pseudonyms of Elizabeth Morison and Frances Lamont. Naturally those who had already been told the story were aware of the authors' identity and it soon became—at all events in academic circles—*secret de Polichinelle*. Many of the criticisms made at the time were based on the fact that dated records of their visits and their researches were not available. In fact the papers were carefully kept. After Miss Jourdain's death Miss Moberly deposited them in the Bodleian Library, and after her own death they were made available for public inspection.[2]

The first book to be devoted to the criticism of *An Adventure* was *The Mystery of Versailles, a Complete Solution*, by J. R. Sturge Whiting, which was published in 1938, when both Miss Moberly and Miss Jourdain were dead. His 'solution', to put it briefly, was that they saw nothing but buildings and scenery that in fact exist, and that the persons they saw were such gardeners and tourists as may be seen about the Petit Trianon at any time.

[1] Miss M. E. Hamilton, Mrs. George Adams, Miss W. M. Mammatt, Mrs. Graham Balfour, Mr. L. Stampa, the Warden of Keble and Mrs. Lock, and others all heard the story in October or November 1901. See their letters in Bodley MS. Eng. misc. d. 249.

[2] The shelf marks are MSS. Eng. misc. d. 249–57, c. 221–4, f. 73–5, and g. 12, 13.

Editor's Preface

The Kiosk they saw was the Belvédère; the bridge they crossed was the Pont du Rocher, and their grotto a part of the existing Rocher. This solution makes an evident appeal to any rationalist; but it should not be forgotten that it was obvious enough to have been considered, and rejected, by Miss Moberly and Miss Jourdain. They always maintained that there was enough of oddity in the appearance and dress in the people they saw to exclude the possibility of their being ordinary attendants and sightseers. The Belvédère, they felt, was not 'their' Kiosk, nor the Rocher bridge 'their' bridge.[1] Anyone who visits the Petit Trianon at leisure can be sure of an interesting hour spent in following their route and in checking their statements against those made by Mr. Sturge Whiting. He studied the documents in the Bodleian and makes no charge whatever against the authors' integrity—indeed his book is warmed by his appreciation of their characters and quality—but he considers that they were credulous and self-deceived.

This solution did not go unchallenged.[2] In 1945 M. Landale Johnston, a retired judge of the Indian Civil Service, published *The Trianon Case, a Review of the Evidence*, which is in fact a defence of *An Adventure* against Mr. Sturge Whiting's aspersions. It is argued with considerable legal acumen.

Still more recently a Frenchman, M. Léon Rey, has discussed *An Adventure* in the *Revue de Paris*.[3] He deprecates all the authors' identification of persons, but accepts their good faith. He adds a curious and significant point. The 'fabrique' which they found in plans and thought was 'their kiosk' was in fact never erected; but their description of the kiosk, with trees behind and round it and a Chinese roof, closely resembles (though they were

[1] *An Adventure*, 1st ed., pp. 36, 48, 67.
[2] Both G. N. M. Tyrrell in his 1942 Myers Memorial Lecture, *Apparitions* (S.P.R. 1943) and W. H. W. Sabine in *Journal of the American Society for Psychical Research*, XLIV, 1950, p. 48, accepted the view that it was a case of hallucination.
[3] 'Une promenade hors du temps', in *Revue de Paris*, December 1952, p. 117.

Editor's Preface

unaware of it) the 'Jeu de Bague' erected in 1776 and demolished at the Revolution.

In the number of the *Journal of the Society for Psychical Research* for July–October, 1953, Mr. G. W. Lambert follows up M. Rey's article in a paper of unusual interest. He identifies the 'kiosk' with a Chinese pavilion designed by Antoine Richard, which, if it were ever erected, was swept away by Mique soon after 1775. He finds a remarkable parallel for the paths the ladies followed, in Richard's *rejected* design for the gardens of the Petit Trianon, made in 1774, which he reproduces. He is inclined to believe that they saw it all in trance, in some relation with the mind of Richard himself. Most of the personages seen he dismisses as 'Monitors' from their normal selves, guarding them from danger in the actual world while they followed the paths of a dream world. The repulsive man at the Kiosk, however, is tentatively interpreted by him as a projection of Richard's memory of the death of his master, Louis XV, from confluent smallpox.

The reader must make up his own mind. I hope that I may have simplified his task by the production of this edition.

Wotton under Edge   JOAN EVANS

Authors' Preface (1911)

It was a great venture to speak openly of a personal experience, and we only do so for the following reasons. First, we prefer that our story, which is known in part to some, should be wholly known as told by ourselves. Secondly, we have collected so much evidence on the subject, that it is possible now to consider it as a whole. Thirdly, conditions are changing at Versailles, and in a short time facts which were unknown, and circumstances which were unusual, may soon become commonplaces, and will lose their force as evidence that some curious psychological conditions must have been present, either in ourselves, or in the place.

It is not our business to explain or to understand—nor do we pretend to understand—what happened to put us into communication with so many true facts, which, nine years ago, no one could have told us of in their entirety. But, in order that others may be able to judge fairly of all the circumstances, we have tried to record exactly what happened as simply and fully as possible.

E. M.
F. L.

23

Authors' Preface (1924)

M[any] years have passed since the incidents occurred which were recorded in *An Adventure*, but our interest in them has not diminished; on the contrary, it has increased. Our view that we had witnessed something unusual yet in accordance with historical fact, generally unknown and quite unknown to us at the time, has been corroborated by fresh evidence.

Finding that on our repeated visits to the Petit Trianon we could never again discover many of the places in which we had been on the first occasion, we took the trouble to ascertain whether the conditions we had known were identical with the historical conditions of the place. This called for first-hand evidence bearing on more than seventy points of minute historical detail, mostly concerning changes in the arrangement of the ground. At that date information on this subject was very scanty. Many of the French histories and biographies of a hundred years ago, now so common, as well as descriptive accounts and illustrations of the place, were published later than our visit in 1901. We had to read original documents. The result of this showed us that everything we had described by word and in writing before the research began was in agreement with the conditions of the place in 1789, many of which had not persisted later than that date. This seemed sufficiently interesting to be recorded, for even if we had been deceived in one or two details, it was difficult to believe that we could have been deceived in all.

One explanation was freely offered to us: it was suggested that preparations for a cinematograph film were taking place whilst we were in the grounds of the Petit Trianon. Though we knew that such a solution did not tally with the facts as we had experienced them, yet before publishing the book in 1911 we consulted the authorities at Versailles about such a possibility. From them we learned definitely that no leave to take photographs for a film was granted during August 1901. Later, we received a letter from the *Château de Versailles* confirming the fact. 'Je n'ai aucun souvenir de scènes historiques photographiées à Versailles ou aux Trianons en août 1901; je suis convaincu qu'il s'agit de la fête donnée au Hameau de Marie Antoinette au mois de juin de cette année-là; et je crains bien qu'il ne soit très difficile d'en trouver des photographies.'

The municipal records show that there had been a fête with historically dressed groups in June 1901, and that some photographs of these groups were taken the following month.[1] A note was added that the fête had taken place at the Hameau. The names of photographers in Paris who were most likely to know about this were supplied to us, but, on enquiry, we were assured that none of them had taken photographs at the Trianon on 10th August 1901, nor did they know of any having been taken at that time.

A definite statement was subsequently made to us that a film was taken by MM. Pathé Frères for a well-known cinematograph 'just at the time' we were at Versailles. A letter to MM. Pathé Frères brought the answer that the film referred to 'a été tourné le jeudi, 24 janvier 1910 à Versailles au Petit Trianon' (not in 1901). Again, more recently, a French journal quoted in several English newspapers, asserted that 'exactly at that date' a film was being taken at the Trianon. The date given was 1905. As we were not in France that year, nor have we ever walked in the Trianon gardens 'par un soir d'automne orageux . . . à la tombée de la nuit', the incident referred to has no bearing on our story.

[1] The photographs in question when shown to us were entirely unlike anything that we had seen.

26

Authors' Preface (1924)

All these suggestions were made in reference to the persons we met. There were eight in all, but never more than two at once. We recognised no one; and while thinking them very French, they were not in such costumes as to remind us of historical personages. Greater and more accurate knowledge, gradually acquired, proved that most of them were in the morning dress of 1789. We have never seen them exactly portrayed in any pictures of costumes of that period.

The most interesting part of our narrative, however, has to do with the change of scenery from what it is now to what it was a hundred years back. Some of it had only existed for sixteen or seventeen years, created by Marie Antoinette and destroyed immediately after her death. The chief features of our experience on that pleasant afternoon were the impressions of exceptional loneliness, and the extreme silence and stillness of the place. These impressions have never been renewed in the same localities.

The Hameau (which we did not see that year) is a part of the grounds having a sheet of water, open glades of trees, and a picturesque background of interesting cottages. It was arranged by Mique, the Queen's architect,[1] and is left untouched save by natural decay. But we were not in that part of the little domain. We were walking on high ground between the Queen's theatre and the smaller lake with the Belvédère. It was a narrow path, having rocks on one side and deeply shaded by trees, completely shutting out any view. For this reason we could not see the Belvédère, or the Temple de l'Amour, or the Rocher bridge which crosses one end of the smaller lake. This overshadowed pathway was (we now know) destroyed by Louis Philippe when he finally levelled the grottos which had been destroyed immediately after the Queen's death. The original formation of it is told in some detail in the gardener's wages-book, which was placed after the King's death in the National Archives at Paris, where we studied it several years after our first visit to Versailles.

[1] Guillotined, 1794.

27

Authors' Preface (1924)

By the recovery in 1903 of Mique's original manuscript plan for the laying out of the Petit Trianon gardens, valuable information has been obtained about the position of the little ravine in the Queen's grotto, exactly confirming our remembered impression. The account given to us by the local authorities of the recovery of this map is a great additional piece of evidence.[1] So, also, is the testimony of the French colonel who with his friend walked with us, in 1913, over that part of the garden. They gave us quite invaluable information about the uniforms worn by the *gardes des portes* in 1789 and about other things. . . .[2]

Though on the afternoon of our first visit to the Petit Trianon there were moments of oppression, yet we were not asleep, nor in a trance, nor even greatly surprised—everything was too natural. Astonishment came later, when we knew more. We were walking briskly during that half-hour or so, talking about other matters, whilst observing with quiet interest our surroundings, which undoubtedly made an indelible impression on our minds. Neither of us had previously made any special study of that period of French history or of the place. We had never heard the latter described, and had not even read Baedeker on the subject. But it is a point of real interest to us that our walk that day and the subsequent researches awoke a very keen interest in French history and literature. It has therefore sometimes been supposed that we knew beforehand the intimate history that we really learned later than that date. But the awakening of a special interest in the history of French thought has made us believe that the incident owed its origin rather to a passing extension of the senses than to any withdrawal of them.

We record these things in order that they may be considered whenever the time shall come when a true explanation of our story may become possible.

[1] Appendix II.
[2] Appendix III. I have omitted five and a half lines referring to Appendix IV of the 1924 edition, which is not included in this edition as it relates the experiences of other, unnamed, persons.

Authors' Preface (1924)

We have to thank many friends in England and France who have kindly communicated with us concerning various points of historical detail, which no ordinary histories of the time and place could supply.

C. ANNE E. MOBERLY

ELEANOR F. JOURDAIN

CHAPTER I

Three Visits to the Petit Trianon

======◁•))∘◇∘◇∘◇∘◇∘((•◁======

MISS MOBERLY'S ACCOUNT OF THE FIRST VISIT TO THE PETIT TRIANON[1]

AUGUST, 1901

After some days of sight-seeing in Paris, to which we were almost strangers, on an August afternoon, 1901,[2] Miss Jourdain and I went to Versailles. We had very hazy ideas as to where it was or what there was to be seen. Both of us thought it might prove to be a dull expedition.[3] We went by train, and walked through the rooms and galleries of the Palace with interest, though we constantly regretted our inability through ignorance to feel properly the charm of the place. My knowledge of French history was limited to the very little I had learnt in the school-room,[4] historical novels and the first volume of Justin McCarthy's *French Revolution*.[5] Over thirty years before my brother had written a prize poem on *Marie Antoinette*, for whom at the time I had felt much enthusiasm. But the German occupation was chiefly in our minds, and Miss Jourdain and I thought and spoke of it several times.

---

[1] This closely follows with very small verbal differences the MS. (B 1) in Bodley MS. Eng. misc. d. 252 fol. 11.

[2] In fact August 10th. J. E.

[3] [We stayed in Paris about three weeks. We remained at home during the mornings and went for expeditions each afternoon, without hurry or fatigue. Note added in 1924 ed.]

[4] [This included Carlyle's *French Revolution* and some general histories of France. Note added in 1924 ed.]

[5] The MS. adds 'which was one of the books Miss Charlotte Yonge and I read aloud to one another the last time that I stayed at Otterbourne'.

31

An Adventure

We sat down in the Salle des Glaces, where a very sweet air was blowing in at the open windows over the flower-beds below, and finding that there was time to spare, I suggested our going to the Petit Trianon. My sole knowledge of it was from a magazine article read as a girl, from which I received a general impression that it was a farm-house where the Queen had amused herself.

Looking at Baedeker's map we saw the sort of direction and that there were two Trianons, and set off. By not asking the way we went an unnecessarily long way round—by the great flights of steps from the fountains and down the central avenue as far as the head of the long pond. The weather had been very hot all the week, but on this day the sky was a little overcast and the sun shaded. There was a lively wind blowing, the woods were looking their best, and we both felt particularly vigorous. It was a most enjoyable walk.

After reaching the beginning of the long water we struck away to the right down a woodland glade until we came obliquely to the other water close to the building which we rightly concluded to be the Grand Trianon. We passed it on our left hand, and came upon[1] a broad green drive perfectly deserted. If we had followed it we should have come immediately to the Petit Trianon, but, not knowing its position, we crossed the drive and went up a lane in front of us. I was surprised that Miss Jourdain did not ask the way from a woman who was shaking a white cloth out of the window of a building at the corner of the lane, but followed, supposing that she knew where she was going to. Talking about England,[2] and mutual acquaintances there, we went up the lane, and then made a sharp turn to the right past some buildings. We looked in at an open doorway and saw the end of a carved staircase, but as no one was about we did not like to go in. There were three paths in front of us, and as we saw two men a little ahead on the centre one, we followed it, and asked them the way. Afterwards we spoke of them as gardeners, because we

---

[1] MS. 'up to'.   [2] MS. 'Oxford'.

3. THE PETIT TRIANON, NORTH SIDE

4. THE BELVÉDÈRE: THE ROCHER TO THE EXTREME LEFT

remembered a wheelbarrow of some kind close by and the look of a pointed spade, but they were really very dignified officials, dressed in long greyish-green coats with small three-cornered hats. They directed us straight on.[1]

We walked briskly forward, talking as before, but from the moment we left the lane an extraordinary depression had come over me, which, in spite of every effort to shake off, steadily deepened. There seemed to be absolutely no reason for it; I was not at all tired, and was becoming more interested in my surroundings. I was anxious that my companion should not discover the sudden gloom upon my spirits, which became quite overpowering on reaching the point where the path ended, being crossed by another, right and left.

In front of us was a wood, within which, and overshadowed by trees, was a light garden kiosk, circular, and like a small bandstand, by which a man was sitting. There was no greensward, but the ground was covered with rough grass and dead leaves as in a wood. The place was so shut in that we could not see beyond it. Everything suddenly looked unnatural, therefore unpleasant; even the trees behind the building seemed to have become flat and lifeless, *like a wood worked in*[2] *tapestry*. There were no effects of light and shade, and no wind stirred the trees. It was all intensely still.

The man sitting close to the kiosk (who had on a cloak and a large shady hat) turned his head and looked at us. This was the culmination of my peculiar sensations, and I felt a moment of genuine alarm. The man's face was most repulsive—its expression odious. His complexion was very dark and rough. I said to Miss Jourdain, 'Which is our way?' but thought 'nothing will induce me to go to the left'. It was a great relief at that moment to hear someone running up to us in breathless haste. Connecting

---

[1] One man looked older than the other. Both were very grave. (Note added in 1924 ed.)

[2] MS. 'on'.

the sound with the gardeners,[1] I turned and ascertained that there was no one on the paths either to the side or behind, but at almost the same moment I suddenly perceived another man quite close to us, behind and rather to the left hand, who had, apparently, just come either over or through the rock (or whatever it was) that shut out the view at the junction of the paths. The suddenness of his appearance was something of a shock.

The second man was distinctly a gentleman; he was tall, with large dark eyes, and had crisp curling black hair under the same large sombrero hat. He was handsome, and the effect of the hair was to make him look like an old picture. His face was glowing red as through great exertion—as though he had come a long way. At first I thought he was sunburnt, but a second look satisfied me that the colour was from heat, not sunburning. He had on a dark cloak wrapped across him like a scarf, one end flying out in his prodigious hurry. He looked greatly excited as he called out to us, 'Mesdames, Mesdames' (or 'Madame' pronounced more as the other), 'il ne faut' (pronounced *fout*)[2] 'pas passer par là.' He then waved his arm, and said with great animation, 'par ici . . . cherchez la maison.'[3]

I was so surprised at his eagerness that I looked up at him again, and to this he responded with a little backward movement and a most peculiar smile. Though I could not follow all he said, it was clear that he was determined that we should go to the right and not to the left. As this fell in with my own wish, I went instantly towards a little bridge on the right, and turning my head to join Miss Jourdain in thanking him, found, to my surprise, that he was not there, but the running began again, and from the sound it was close beside us.

Silently we passed over the small rustic bridge which crossed a tiny ravine. So close to us when on the bridge that we could have

[1] MS. 'garden officials'.   [2] MS. 'fou'.
[3] The man said a great deal more which we could not catch. [He was young and active and greatly excited. Note added in 1924 ed.]

Three Visits to the Petit Trianon

touched it with our right hands, a thread-like cascade fell from a height down a green pretty bank, where ferns grew between stones. Where the little trickle of water went to I did not see, but it gave me the impression that we were near other water, though I saw none.

Beyond the little bridge our pathway led under trees; it skirted a narrow meadow of long grass bounded on the farther side by trees, and very much overshadowed by trees growing in it. This gave the whole place a sombre look suggestive of dampness, and shut out the view of the house until we were close to it. The house was a square, solidly built small country house—quite different from what I expected. The long windows looking north into the English garden (where we were) were shuttered. There was a terrace round the north and west sides of the house, and on the rough grass, which grew quite up to the terrace, and with her back to it, a lady was sitting, holding out a paper as though to look at it at arm's-length. I supposed her to be sketching, and to have brought her own camp-stool. It seemed as though she must be making a study of trees, for they grew close in front of her, and there seemed to be nothing else to sketch. She saw us, and when we passed close by on her left hand, she turned and looked full at us. It was not a young face, and (though rather pretty) it did not attract me. She had on a shady white hat perched on a good deal of fair hair that fluffed round her forehead. Her light summer dress was arranged on her shoulders in handkerchief fashion, and there was a little line of either green or gold near the edge of the handkerchief, which showed me that it was *over*, not tucked *into*, her bodice, which was cut low. Her dress was long-waisted, with a good deal of fullness in the skirt, which seemed to be short. I thought she was a tourist, but that her dress was old-fashioned and rather unusual (though people were wearing fichu bodices that summer). I looked straight at her; but some indescribable feeling made me turn away annoyed at her being there.

35

An Adventure

We went up the steps on to the terrace, my impression being that they led up direct from the English garden; but I was beginning to feel as though we were walking in a dream—the stillness and oppressiveness were so unnatural. Again I saw the lady, this time from behind, and noticed that her fichu was pale green. It was rather a relief to me that Miss Jourdain did not propose to ask her whether we could enter the house from that side.

We crossed the terrace to the south-west corner and looked over into the *cour d'honneur*;[1] and then turned back, and seeing[2] that one of the long windows overlooking the French garden was unshuttered, we were going towards it when we were interrupted. The terrace was prolonged at right angles in front of what seemed to be a second house. The door of it suddenly opened, and a young man stepped out on to the terrace, banging the door behind him. He had the jaunty manner of a footman, but no livery, and called to us, saying that the way into the house was by the *cour d'honneur*,[1] and offered to show us the way round. He looked inquisitively amused as he walked by us down the French garden till we came to an entrance into the front drive. We came out sufficiently[3] near the first lane we had been in to make me wonder why the garden officials had not directed us back instead of telling us to go forward.

When we were in the front entrance hall we were kept waiting for the arrival of a merry French wedding-party. They walked arm-in-arm in a long procession round the rooms, and we were at the back—too far off from the guide to hear much of his story. We were very much interested, and felt quite lively again. Coming out of the *cour d'honneur*[1] we took a little carriage which was standing there, and drove back to the Hôtel des Réservoirs in Versailles, where we had tea;[4] but we were neither of us inclined to talk, and did not mention any of the events of the afternoon.

[1] MS. 'courtyard'.   [2] MS. 'fancying'.   [3] MS. 'so'.
[4] I remember that on account of the wind I put on my coat.

36

Three Visits to the Petit Trianon

After tea we walked back to the station, looking on the way for the Tennis Court.

On the way back to Paris the setting sun at last burst out from under the clouds, bathing the distant Versailles woods in glowing light—Valérien standing out in front, a mass of deep purple. Again and again the thought returned[1]—Was Marie Antoinette really much at Trianon, and did she see it for the last time long before the fatal drive to Paris accompanied by the mob?

For a whole week we never alluded to that afternoon, nor did I think about it until I began writing a descriptive letter of our expeditions of the week before. As the scenes came back one by one, the same sensation of dreamy unnatural oppression came over me so strongly that I stopped writing, and said to Miss Jourdain, 'Do you think that the Petit Trianon is haunted?' Her answer was prompt, 'Yes, I do.' I asked her where she felt it, and she said, 'In the garden where we met the two men, but not only there.' She then described her feeling of depression and anxiety which began at the same point as it did with me, and how she tried not to let me know it. Talking it over we fully realised, for the first time, the theatrical appearance of the man who spoke to us, the inappropriateness of the wrapped cloak on a warm summer afternoon, the unaccountableness of his coming and going, the excited running which seemed to begin and end close to us, and yet always out of sight, and the extreme earnestness with which he desired us to go one way and not another. I said that the thought had crossed[2] my mind that the two men were going to fight a duel, and that they were waiting until we were gone. Miss Jourdain owned to having disliked[3] the thought of passing the man of the kiosk.

We did not speak again of the incident during my stay in Paris, though we visited the Conciergerie prisons, and the tombs of Louis XVI and Marie Antoinette at Saint-Denis, where all was clear and fresh and natural.

[1] MS. 'occurred'.   [2] MS. 'come into'.   [3] MS. 'disliking'.

An Adventure

Three months later Miss Jourdain came to stay with me,[1] and on Sunday, 10th November, 1901, we returned to the subject, and I said, 'If we had known that a lady was sitting so near us sketching it would have made all the difference, for we should have asked[2] the way.' She replied that she had seen no lady. I reminded her of the person sitting under the terrace; but Miss Jourdain declared that there was no one there. I exclaimed that it was impossible that she should not have seen the individual, for we were walking side by side and went[3] straight up to her, passed her and looked down upon her from the terrace. It was inconceivable to us both that she should not have seen the lady, but the fact was clear[4] that Miss Jourdain had not done so,[5] though we had both been rather on the look-out for someone who would reassure us as to whether we were trespassing or not.

Finding that we had a new element of mystery, and doubting how far we had seen any of the same things, we resolved to write down independent accounts of our expedition to Trianon, read up its history, and make every enquiry about the place. Miss Jourdain returned to her school[6] the same evening, and two days later I received from her a very interesting letter, giving the result of her first enquiries.

November, 1901   C.A.E.M.

[1] MS. 'at Oxford'.   [2] MS. 'asked her'.
[3] MS. 'walked'.   [4] MS. 'quite certain'.
[5] MS. 'had been unconscious of her presence'.
[6] MS. 'to Watford'.

Three Visits to the Petit Trianon

MISS JOURDAIN'S ACCOUNT OF HER FIRST VISIT TO THE PETIT TRIANON IN 1901[1]

AUGUST, 1901

In the summer of 1900 I stayed in Paris for the first time, and in the course of that summer took a flat and furnished it, intending to place a French lady there in charge of my elder schoolgirls.[2] Paris was quite new to me, and beyond seeing the picture galleries and one or two churches I made no expeditions except to shops, for the Exhibition of 1900 was going on, and all my free time was spent in seeing it with my French friends. The next summer, however, 1901, when, after several months at my school in England, I came back to Paris, it was to take the first opportunity possible of having a visitor to stay there: and I asked Miss Moberly to come with me.

Miss Moberly suggested our seeing the historic part of Paris in something like chronological order, and I looked forward to seeing it practically for the first time with her. We decided to go to Versailles one day, though rather reluctantly, as we felt it was diverging from our plan to go there too soon. I did not know what to expect, as my ignorance of the place and its significance was extreme. So we looked up general directions in Baedeker, and trusted to finding our way at the time.

After spending some time in the Palace, we went down by the terrace[3] and struck to the right to find the Petit Trianon. We walked for some distance down a wooded alley, and then came upon the buildings of the Grand Trianon, before which we did not delay. We went on in the direction of the Petit Trianon, but just before reaching what we knew afterwards to be the main entrance I saw a gate leading to a path cut deep below the level of

[1] This closely follows the account (B2) in Bodley MS. Eng. misc. d. 252 fol. 21.
[2] MS. 'schoolgirls from Watford'.
[3] MS. 'terraces'.

the ground above, and as the way was open and had the look of an entrance that was used, I said, 'Shall we try this path? it must lead to the house;' and we followed it. To our right we saw some farm-buildings looking empty and deserted; implements (among others a plough) were lying about; we looked in, but saw no one. The impression was saddening, but it was not until we reached the crest of the rising ground where there was a garden that I began to feel as if we had lost our way, and as if something were wrong. There were two men there in official dress (greenish in colour), with something in their hands; it might have been a staff. A wheelbarrow and some other gardening tools[1] were near them. They told us, in answer to my enquiry, to go straight on. I remembered repeating my question, because they answered in a seemingly casual and mechanical way, but only got the same answer in the same manner. As we were standing there I saw to the right of us a detached solidly built cottage, with stone steps at the door. A woman and a girl were standing at the doorway, and I particularly noticed their unusual dress: both wore white kerchiefs tucked into the bodice, and the girl's dress, though she looked thirteen or fourteen only, was down to her ankles. The woman was passing a jug to the girl, who wore a close white cap.[2]

Following the directions of the two men we walked on: but the path pointed out to us seemed to lead away from where we imagined the Petit Trianon to be; and there was a feeling of depression and loneliness about the place. I began to feel as if I were walking in my sleep; the heavy dreaminess was oppressive. At last we came upon a path crossing ours, and saw in front of us a building consisting of some columns roofed in, and set back in

[1] MS. 'tool'.
[2] The woman was standing on the steps, bending slightly forward, holding a jug in her hand. The girl was looking up at her from below with her hands raised, but nothing in them. She might have been just going to take the jug or have just given it up. Her light brown hair escaped from under her cap. I remember that both seemed to pause for an instant, as in a *tableau vivant*; but we passed on, and I did not see the end.

the trees. Seated on the steps was a man with a heavy black cloak round his shoulders, and wearing a slouch hat. At that moment the eerie feeling which had begun in the garden culminated in a definite impression of something uncanny and fear inspiring. The man slowly turned his face, which was marked by smallpox: his complexion was very dark. The expression was very evil and yet unseeing, and though I did not feel that he was looking particularly at us, I felt a repugnance to going past him. But I did not wish to show the feeling, which I thought was meaningless, and we talked about the best way to turn, and decided to go to the right.

Suddenly we heard a man running behind us: he shouted, 'Mesdames, mesdames,' and when I turned he said in an accent that seemed to me unusual that our way lay in another direction. 'Il ne faut' (pronounced *fout*)[1] 'pas passer par là.' He then made a gesture, adding, 'par ici . . . cherchez la maison.'[2] Though we were surprised to be addressed, we were glad of the direction, and I thanked him. The man ran off with a curious smile on his face: the running ceased as abruptly as it had begun, not far from where we stood. I remember that the man was young-looking, with a florid complexion and rather long dark hair. I do not remember the dress, except that the material was dark and heavy, and that the man wore buckled shoes.[3]

We walked on, crossing a small bridge that went across a green bank high on our right hand and shelving down below as to a very small overshadowed pool of water glimmering some way off. A tiny stream descended from above us, so small as to seem to lose itself before reaching the little pool. We then followed a narrow path till almost immediately we came upon the English

---

[1] MS. 'fou'.

[2] Note in MS.: 'By an unusual accent I mean that nearly every word had a different quality of vowel sound, for example, in the first word, though I suppose he meant "Mesdames", it sounded like "Madame" with the consonant doubled.'

[3] The last seven words are not in the MS.

garden front of the Petit Trianon. The place was deserted; but as we approached the terrace I remember drawing my skirt away with a feeling as though someone were near and I had to make room, and then wondering why I did it. While we were on the terrace a boy came out of the door of a second building which opened on it, and I still have the sound in my ears of his slamming it behind him. He directed us to go round to the other entrance, and, seeing us hesitate, with the peculiar smile of suppressed mockery offered to show us the way. We passed through the French garden, part of which was walled in by trees. The feeling of dreariness was very strong there, and continued till we actually reached the front entrance to the Petit Trianon and looked round the rooms in the wake of a French wedding-party. Afterwards we drove back to the Rue des Réservoirs.

The impression returned to me at intervals during the week that followed, but I did not speak of it until Miss Moberly asked me if I thought the Petit Trianon was haunted, and I said Yes. Then, too, the inconsistency of the dress and behaviour of the man with an August afternoon at Versailles struck me. We had only this one conversation about the two men. Nothing else passed between us in Paris.

It was not till three months later, when I was staying[1] with her, that Miss Moberly casually mentioned the lady, and almost refused to believe that I had not seen her. How that happened was quite inexplicable to me, for I believed myself to be looking about on all sides, and it was not so much that I did not remember her as that I could have said no one was there. But as she said it I remembered my impression at the moment of there being more people than I could see, though I did not tell her this.

The same evening, 10th November, 1901, I returned to my school near London.[2] Curiously enough the next morning I had to give one of a set of lessons on the French Revolution for the

[1] MS. 'staying at St. Hugh's Hall'.
[2] MS. 'to Watford'.

Three Visits to the Petit Trianon

Higher Certificate, and it struck me for the first time with great interest that the 10th of August had a special significance in French history, and that we had been at Trianon on the anniversary of the day.

That evening, when I was preparing to write down my experiences, a French friend[1] whose home was in Paris came into my room, and I asked her, just on the chance, if she knew any story about the haunting of the Petit Trianon. (I had not mentioned our story to her before, nor indeed to anyone.) She said directly that she remembered hearing from friends[2] at Versailles that on a certain day in August Marie Antoinette is regularly seen sitting outside the garden front at[3] the Petit Trianon, with a light flapping hat and a pink dress. More than this, that the place, especially the farm, the garden, and the path by the water, are peopled with those who used to be with her there; in fact that all the occupants and amusements reproduce themselves there for a day and a night. I then told her our story, and when I quoted the words that the man spoke to us, and imitated as well as I could his accent, she immediately said that it was the Austrian pronunciation of French. I had privately thought that he spoke old[4] French. Immediately afterwards I wrote and told this to Miss Moberly.

November, 1901   E.F.J.

On receiving Miss Jourdain's letter I turned to[5] my diary to see on what Saturday in August it was that we had visited Versailles, and looked up[6] the history to find out to what event she alluded. On 10th August 1792[7] the Tuileries was sacked.

---

[1] [Mademoiselle Ménégoz. J.E.] MS. Mlle. M. daughter of Professor M.

[2] MS. 'her friends the J (the rest obliterated)'.

[3] MS. 'of'.

[4] By 'old' I mean old or unusual forms, perhaps surviving in provincial French.

[5] MS. 'I first looked in'.

[6] MS. 'and then began to look up'.

[7] The subsequent pages of the MS. give a more detailed account of these historical events.

An Adventure

The royal family escaped in the early morning to the Hall of the Assembly, where they were penned up for many hours hearing themselves practically deposed, and within sound of the massacre of their servants and of the Swiss Guards at the Tuileries. From the Hall the King and Queen were taken to the Temple.

We wondered whether[1] we had inadvertently entered within an act of the Queen's memory when alive, and whether this explained our curious sensation of being completely *shut in* and oppressed. What more likely, we thought, than that[2] during those hours in the Hall of the Assembly, or in the Conciergerie, she had gone back in such vivid memory to other Augusts spent at Trianon[3] that some impress of it was imparted to the place? Some pictures[4] which were shown to me proved that the outdoor dress of the gentlemen at Court[5] had been a large hat[6] and cloak, and that the ladies wore long-waisted bodices, with full gathered short skirts, fichus, and hats.

I told the story to my brother, and we heartily agreed that, as a rule, such stories made no impression at all upon us, because we always believed that, if only the persons involved would take the trouble to investigate them thoroughly and honestly for themselves, they could be quite naturally explained. We agreed that such a story as ours had very little value without more proof of reality than it had, but that as there were one or two interesting points in it, it would be best to sift the matter quietly, lest others should make more of them than they deserved. He suggested lightly and in fun that perhaps we had seen the Queen as

[1] MS. 'our first theory was that'.
[2] MS. 'Either during the terrible 18 hours in the Hall'.
[3] MS. 'and to the last sad visit'.
[4] MS. 'The idea of *memory* received unexpected confirmation in December 1901 by my being shown an old picture of the woods at Versailles in the Christmas number of the *Pall Mall Magazine* of 1893, which brought back the flattened look of the trees at Trianon as I had seen them for a moment. Other pictures showed that the outdoor dress . . .'
[5] MS. 'at Trianon'.   [6] MS. 'slouch hat'.

Three Visits to the Petit Trianon

she thought of herself, and that it would be interesting to know whether the dress described was the one she had on at the time of her *rêverie*, or whether it was one she recollected having worn at an earlier date. My brother also enquired whether we were quite sure that the last man we had seen (who came out of the side building), as well as the wedding-party, were all real persons. I assured him with great amusement that we had not the smallest doubt as to the reality of them all.[1]

As Miss Jourdain was going to Paris for the Christmas holidays, I wrote and asked her to take any opportunity she might have to see the place again, and to make a plan of the paths and the buildings; for the guide-books spoke of the Temple de l'Amour and the Belvédère, and I thought one of them might prove to be our kiosk.

C.A.E.M.

MISS JOURDAIN'S ACCOUNT OF HER SECOND VISIT TO THE PETIT TRIANON[2]

JANUARY, 1902

On 2nd January 1902, I went for the second time to Versailles. It was a cold and wet day, but I was anxious not to be deterred by that, as it was likely to be my only possible day that winter. This time I drove straight to the Petit Trianon, passing the Grand Trianon, near which I could see the path up which we had walked in August. I went, however, to the regular entrance, thinking I would go at once to the Temple de l'Amour, even if I had time to go no further. To the right of the courtyard was a door in the wall; it led to the Hameau de la Reine and to the gardens. I took this path and came to the Temple de l'Amour, which was *not* the building we had passed in the summer. There

---

[1] This paragraph occurs later in the MS., fol. 34, with some slight modifications.

[2] [Checked from Bodley MS. Eng. misc. d. 252 fol. 35. J.E.]

was, so far, none of the eerie feeling we had experienced in August. But on crossing a bridge to go to the Hameau the old feeling returned in full force: it was as if I had crossed a line and was suddenly in a circle of influence. To the left I saw a tract of park-like ground, the trees bare and very scanty. I noticed a cart being filled with sticks by two labourers, and thought I could go to them for directions if I lost my way. The men wore tunics and capes with pointed hoods of bright colours, a sort of terra-cotta red and deep blue.[1] I turned aside for an instant—not more —to look at the Hameau, and when I looked back men and cart were completely out of sight, and this surprised me, as I could see a long way in every direction and their total disappearance in so short a time seemed unaccountable. And though I had seen the men in the act of loading the cart with sticks, I could not see any trace of them on the ground, either at the time or afterwards; but I did not dwell upon any part of the incident, but went on to the Hameau. The houses were all built near a sheet of water, and the old oppressive feeling of the last year was noticeable, especially under the balcony of the Maison de la Reine, and near a window in what I afterwards found to be the Laiterie. I really felt a great reluctance to go near the window or look in, and when I did so I found it shuttered inside.

Coming away from the Hameau I at last reached a building, which I knew from my plan to be the smaller Orangerie; then, meaning to go to the Belvédère, I turned back by mistake into the park and found myself in a wood so thick that though I had turned towards the Hameau I could not see it. Before I entered I looked across an open space towards a belt of trees to the left of the Hameau, some way off, and noticed a man, cloaked like those we had seen before, slip swiftly through the line of trees. His movement attracted my attention because it was remarkable: he seemed to be among the trees, and yet the straightness of his course suggested that they were independent of one another.

[1] One man wore red, the other blue; the colours were not mixed.

Three Visits to the Petit Trianon

I was puzzling my way among the maze of paths in the wood, when I heard a rustling behind me which made me wonder why people in silk dresses came out on such a wet day; and I said to myself, 'just like French people'. I turned sharply round to see who they were, but saw no one, and then all in a moment I had the same feeling as by the terrace in the summer, only in a much greater degree; it was as though I were closed in by a group of people who already filled the path, coming from behind and passing me. At one moment there seemed really no room for me. I heard some women's voices talking French, and caught the words 'Monsieur et Madame' said close to my ear. The crowd got scarce and drifted away, and then faint music, as of a band not far off, was audible. It was playing very light music with a good deal of repetition in it. Both voices and music were diminished in tone, as in a phonograph, unnaturally. The pitch of the band was lower than usual. The sounds were intermittent, and once more I felt the swish of a dress close by me.

I looked at the map which I had with me, but whenever I settled which path to take I felt impelled to go by another. After turning backwards and forwards many times I at last found myself back at the Orangerie, and was overtaken by a gardener. I asked him where I should find the Queen's grotto, that had been mentioned in de Nolhac's book which I had procured while in Paris. He gave me a very vague direction, adding that it was quite impossible to find one's way about the park unless one had been brought up in the place, and so used to it that 'personne ne pourrait vous tromper'. The expression specially impressed me because of the experience I had just had in the wood. He pointed out the way and left me.[1] The path led past the Belvédère,

---

[1] I thought this gardener did not look like a Frenchman; he had more the air of an Englishman. He had hair on his face, a grizzled beard, and was large and loosely made. His height was very uncommon and he seemed to be of immense strength. His arms were long and very muscular: I noticed that even through the sleeves of his jersey. In answer to my question about the grotto, he merely told me to follow the path I was on.

which I took for granted was the building we had seen in August, for coming upon it from behind all the water was hidden from me. I made my way from there to the French garden without noticing the paths I took.

On my return to Versailles I made careful enquiries as to whether the band had been playing there that day, but was told that though it was the usual day of the week, it had not played because it had played the day before, being New Year's Day.

I told my French friends of my walk, and they said that there was a tradition of Marie Antoinette having been seen making butter within the Laiterie, and for that reason it was shuttered. A second tradition they mentioned interested me very much. It was that on October 5th 1789—which was the last day on which Marie Antoinette went to Trianon—she was sitting there in her grotto, and saw a page running towards her, bringing the letter from the minister at the Palace to say that the mob from Paris would be at the gates in an hour's time. The story went on that she impulsively proposed walking straight back to the Palace by the short cut through the trees. He would not allow it; but begged her to go to the 'maison' to wait whilst he fetched the carriage by which she was generally conveyed back through the Park, and that he ran off to order it.

January, 1902.   E.F.J.

1902–1904

During the next two years nothing occurred to throw light on the story. We tried to get corroboration of the tradition and to find out exact routes, but were not very successful. The person living in Versailles[1] to whom we had been directed as having related the tradition of the Queen's being at Trianon on 5th October 1789, was unable to remember anything at all about it. The photographs of the Belvédère made it clear that it was not

---

[1] [Further details about these enquiries are given in the MS but the names have been obliterated. J.E.]

48

identical with the kiosk. On the many occasions on which Miss Jourdain went to the Trianon she could never again find the places—not even the wood in which she had been. She assured me that the place was entirely different and commonplace; the distances were much less than we had imagined;[1] that the ground was so open and bare that the house and the Hameau were in full view of one another, and that there was nothing unnatural about the trees nor could they have been altered in so short a time.

Miss Jourdain brought back pictures of the place as it is now, amongst others some of the Belvédère, which was *not* the kiosk. Excepting in the fact that it was circular there was no likeness. She agreed with me that the kiosk was not a closed stone building, but was small and lightly made, standing in a wood and not on a hill, that there was no green mound, nor any sheet of water at its foot; so characteristic of the Belvédère even in the old pictures of it. The only bridge apparently was Le Rocher[2] which had no resemblance to ours, being much larger, more conspicuous, and over one end of the open lake. We knew that changes in the bridges and the disposition of the water might easily have been made in the course of two years, and I had no doubt that when we could go there together we should find out where we had been.

One point of interest was made; in January 1904 Miss Jourdain went to the Comédie Française to see *Le Barbier de Séville*, and saw that the Alguazils standing round were dressed exactly like our garden officials, with the addition of scarlet stockings. The special interest of this was that she had not been able to find that

[1] A note, undated, by Miss Jourdain has been added to the MS here. 'I should like to emphasise this. On my first two visits to the Trianon (but never again) the difficulty of getting over the ground seemed extreme and the distances great. There was a feeling that time was against us, and, especially in the winter (1902) as if some obstacle—as in a bad dream—prevented me from moving forward easily to the places I saw in front of me. I have been to Trianon many times since but have never felt anything of the same kind again. E. J. Jourdain.'

[2] We called it the Rocher bridge because of the rock over it and also because it was in the part of the garden called Le Rocher.

any green uniforms or small three-cornered hats were worn at the Trianon now. The Comédie Française is the descendant of the Royal Private Theatre, and the old royal liveries worn by the subordinate officials (who were, in old times, the royal servants) are carefully reproduced at it. Almaviva had the ordinary outdoor dress of a French gentleman of the period, a dark cloak and a large Spanish hat.

We read everything concerning Marie Antoinette that we could reach, and began to have some knowledge of her history.[1]

No pictures of the Queen were like the lady I saw. In all of them the face was not square enough and the nose was too long and aquiline. But on turning over the pages of Desjardins' *Petit Trianon* we came upon Wertmüller's picture of her and I exclaimed that it really brought back the face I had seen. Some weeks after I read the book carefully and found these words:[2] 'Ce tableau fut assez mal accueilli des critiques contemporains qui le trouvèrent froid, sans majesté, sans grâce. Pour la postérité, au contraire, il a le plus grand mérite; celui de la ressemblance. Au dire de Madame Campan, il n'existe de bon portrait de la reine que cette toile de Wertmüller et celle que Madame Lebrun peignit en 1787. . . .'[3]

C.A.E.M.

MISS MOBERLY'S ACCOUNT OF HER SECOND VISIT TO THE PETIT TRIANON IN 1904

On Monday, 4th July 1904, Miss Jourdain and I went to the Trianon. We were accompanied by Mademoiselle ──, who had not heard our story. On the Saturday of the same week (9th July) we went again unaccompanied. Both days were brilliant and hot.

[1] [The MS. contains a long list of books.]
[2] p. 292.
[3] The MS. here continues with an account of other investigations and discoveries which in the first edition (and here) are included under 'Results of Research' below.

Three Visits to the Petit Trianon

On both occasions the dust, glare, trams, comers and goers, were entirely different from the quietness and solitude of our former visit in 1901. We went up the same lane as before and turned to the right on reaching the building, which we had now learnt to call the *logement du Corps de Garde*. From this point everything was changed. We spent a long time looking for the old paths and the kiosk. Not only was there no trace of them, but the distances were contracted and all seemed on a smaller scale than I recollected. We came directly to the gardener's house, (quite different in appearance from the cottage described by Miss Jourdain), in front of which was a parterre of flower-beds, and a smooth lawn of many years' careful tendance. It did not seem to be the place where we had met the garden officials.

The little bridge over the green ravine could not be found. The large bridge with the *rocher* over it crossing one side of the lake at the foot of the Belvédère mound was not at all like it. The trees were quite natural, and seemed to have been a good deal cleared out.

The English garden in front of the house was not shaded by many trees and we could see the house and the Hameau from almost every point. Instead of a much-shaded rough meadow continuing up to the wall of the terrace, there is now a broad gravel sweep beneath it, and the trees on the grass are gone. Exactly where the 'lady' was sitting we found a large rhododendron bush of, apparently, many years' growth.

To add to the impossibility of recalling our first visit, we came across in every corner groups of noisy merry people walking or sitting in the shade. Garden seats placed everywhere and stalls for fruit and lemonade took away from any idea of desolation. The commonplace, everyday unhistorical atmosphere was totally inconsistent with the air of silent mystery by which we had been so much oppressed. Though for more than two years Miss Jourdain had assured me of the change, I had not expected such a complete disillusionment.

An Adventure

One thing struck us greatly—people went wherever they liked and no one would think of interfering to show the way, or to prevent anyone from going in any direction. We could, and did, search the place at our pleasure.

Not far from where we must have been accosted by the running man we found a very small grotto and climbed down and passed through it, but it was a very small affair and not the one that is now said to be the traditional Queen's grotto.

We went to the Hameau, and walked from there to the small Orangerie. I asked Miss Jourdain to point out the paths she had followed in the winter of 1902. But it was impossible for there were no woods at all in that part and such paths as there are now are perfectly visible, even in summer, from one another, being merely in the open park.

We asked a gardener sweeping one of the paths whether that part of the grounds had been at any time a thick wood. He said it had, but could not give us any date beyond the fact that it was before his time—more than twenty years ago.

On our return to Versailles we went to a bookseller's shop (Bernard, 17 rue Hoche) and asked whether he had any maps or views of the Trianon as it had been 'dans le temps'. He showed us a single copy (which he would not part with) of the Jeu de Bague. We saw at once that the central building had some likeness to our kiosk, but the rest of it was not like, and its position unsuitable for our purpose. We enquired about green uniforms of the garden officials, and he emphatically denied their existence. He said 'green was one of the colours of the royal liveries', and when we answered that three years before persons in long green coats had directed us in the gardens, he spoke of it as 'impossible—unless', he added, 'they were masqueraders.' One of the *gardiens* of the Palace also said that green was a royal livery and that now only the President had the right to use it on certain occasions.

We asked how long the gardens had been thrown open to the

Three Visits to the Petit Trianon

public and people allowed to wander everywhere, and were told that 'it had been so for *years*', and this evidently implied a great many years.

C.A.E.M.
E.F.J.

CHAPTER II

Results of Research

━━━━━━━━━━━━━━━━━━━━━━

THE PLOUGH

THE first incident in our expedition to Trianon in 1901 was that, after passing the *logement du corps de garde*, a small hand-plough was seen by Miss Jourdain lying on the ground not far from some wide-open gates in an old wall opposite us, through which we could see the stems of a grove of trees, and a drive leading through it.

In 1905 she was told by a gardener that no plough was kept at Trianon; there was no need of one, as the Government only required the lawns, walks, water, trees and flowers to be kept up.

In 1908 another gardener told us both that ploughs have entirely altered in character since the Revolution, and it was not likely that the old type would be seen anywhere in France now.

It would seem that no plough was used ordinarily at Trianon even in old days, for amongst a list of tools bought for the gardeners from 1780–1789 there is no mention of a plough.[1]

We learned, in 1905, from Desjardins' book, that throughout the reign of Louis XVI an old plough used in his predecessor's reign had been preserved at the Petit Trianon and sold with the King's other properties during the Revolution.[2]

A picture of this identical plough, procured in 1907, showed

[1] *Archives Nationales* O[1], 1878.
[2] G. A. Desjardins, *Le Petit Trianon*, 1885, p. 15; Rocheterie, *Histoire de Marie Antoinette*, pp. 289, 290, vol. i.

that it had handles like the one seen in 1901, but the ploughshare was hidden in the ground and could not be compared.[1]

In the old map of 1783[2] there is ploughed land where, later, the Hameau was built and the sheet of water placed: but there is none in the later maps, nor any now to be seen in the grounds.

THE GUARDS

The second event was our meeting with two dignified thoughtful-looking officials, dressed in long green coats and three-cornered hats, holding something in their hands which Miss Jourdain wrote of in 1901 as possibly being staves. In response to our enquiry for the Petit Trianon they coldly directed us forward.

There are no officials so dressed at Trianon now. At present they wear black, with tricolour rosettes in their hats; in summer they have white trousers.

In 1904 we were told by fully informed persons at Versailles that it was 'impossible' that we should have seen such uniforms, 'unless they were worn by masqueraders,' for green was a royal livery, and no one wore it now at Trianon.[3]

Supposing them to have been masqueraders, the dress may have been that of *gardes de la porte*. The ceremonial overdress of the *gardes de la porte*, as was that of part of the *gardes du corps* (*gardes de la Manche*), was green, with gold and silver embroidery and red stockings; they carried halberds.[4] But the officers had *galon* instead of embroidery, and no red stockings; they carried an ebony cane with an ivory ball.[5]

[1] In the Bibliothèque Nationale.
[2] [Mique's map, copied by Contant de la Motte. Note added in 1924 ed.] [This is reproduced in part in Plates II and III.—J.E.]
[3] [The King's livery was blue and silver; the Queen's was scarlet and gold. 'L'habit de Trianon était écarlate, avec une veste à fond blanc, bordée de fil d'or. C'est toujours, comme on voit, la livrée de la reine.' Even the King sometimes came to Trianon in it.—Desjardins, pp. 81, 259, 297. Note added in 1924 ed.]
[4] Picture of a 'Garde de la Porte du Roi Louis XV, dite de la Manche, d'après une gravure de Chevilet.'—R. Jacquemin.
[5] *Souvenirs d'un Page, le comte d'Hezecques*, 1895, pp. 130–134. He says that their underdress was blue.)

An Adventure

The livery of the comte d'Artois, who was *colonel-général* of the *gardes Suisses,* was green; and those of the *gardes du corps* and *Suisses* who were in his service had green uniforms.[1]

There is evidence of a much quieter dress without even *galon,* called the 'petite livrée', which was probably green, as it was worn by the *Suisses, piqueurs, gardes de la porte,* and the *garçons jardiniers.*[2] The traditional dress of those royal servants who filled the minor parts in the Royal Theatre at Versailles is still to be seen at the acting of the *Barbier de Séville* in the Comédie Française, which is the descendant of the Royal Theatre. This dress (except for the added red stockings) is the same as the one we saw in 1901.

In 1908 we learned that the *porte du jardinier* at the Petit Trianon was always guarded 'dans le temps', and that on 5th October 1789 the guards were two of the three Bersy brothers, who, with Bréval, were generally on duty whenever the Queen was in residence at Trianon. From their writing and spelling they were evidently well educated.[3] They had the title of *garçons jardiniers de la Chambre,* and they are said to have been stationed in *'la pépinière proche la maison'.*[4] The most ancient *pépinière* was close to the gardener's house.

COTTAGE, WOMAN, AND GIRL

Whilst speaking to the two men, Miss Jourdain observed on her right hand a solidly built cottage with stone steps, on which a woman in old-fashioned dress was standing, handing something to a girl of about thirteen or fourteen, who wore a white cap and skirts nearly reaching to her ankles.

In 1904, she saw a picture resembling this cottage in its general appearance in the *Album de Trianon* at the Bibliothèque Nationale. In 1908, she and a friend discovered such a cottage (more than one) within the gates, which were not far from the

[1] *Ibid.,* p. 137.
[2] *Arch. Nat.* O[1], 1883.
[3] *Arch. Nat.* O[1], 1878 and 1880.
[4] *Ibid.,* 1878 and 1880.

place where she had seen the plough. These cottages were not in the right position for our experience in 1901, but the type was the same.

In 1907 we discovered from the map of 1783 that there was a building, not now in existence, placed against the wall (outside) of the gardener's yard between the *ruelle* and the *porte du jardinier* near the reservoir.[1] This building would be exactly in the right place for Miss Jourdain's cottage.

In September, 1910, we saw from marks on this wall that a building might have stood here; for the cornice of the wall is broken into, and there seems to be a perpendicular line from it to the ground visible through the plaster. A photograph shows this.

If the girl seen were the 'Marion' of Madame Julie Lavergne's story (first read in 1906), she would have been fourteen years old in 1789, and her mother was then alive.[2] Her father's house would have been near the reservoir and not within the locked gates of the enclosure, for she let herself out at night by an open window.[3] All this would suit the position of the building in the map.

THE KIOSK

On our entrance into the English garden in 1901, we found our path crossed by another, beyond which, in front of us but rather to the left hand, stood a small circular building having pillars and a low surrounding wall. It was on rough uneven ground, and was over-shadowed by trees.

Repeated searches by ourselves and others have failed to discover this building.

[In 1906 the authorities at Versailles showed us an old map

[1] [Map by Contant de la Motte. Note added in 1924 ed.]

[2] [Marion's mother died shortly before 1793. In 1793 Marion was chosen by the Versailles Republican Club to personate the local Goddess of Reason. Horrified at the prospect, the night before the installation on the altar of the Versailles Notre Dame she so disfigured her face with scratches from a thorn branch that she never completely lost the marks. —[Julie] Lavergne, *Légendes de Trianon*, [Lille, n.d., *c.* 1890], p. 97. Note added in 1924 ed.]

[3] *Ibid.*, pp. 89, 96.

An Adventure

'*vers* 1783' and pointed to the site of an erection and later of a *monticule*, both of which had now disappeared.

The position was right for our kiosk between the Orangerie and the little theatre.]¹

In September, 1908, Miss Jourdain found in the archives a paper (without signature or date) giving the estimate for a 'ruine' having seven Ionic columns, walls, and a dome roof.² (A 'ruine' seems only to mean a copy of an older building.)³ If the walls of this building were low it would correspond in appearance with our recollection of the kiosk. This 'ruine' is said to have formed a 'naissance de la rivière', suggesting its position above the small lake which fed the principal river.⁴ A piece of old water pipe is still to be seen on the north-western side of the small lake.

If this 'ruine' and two others of those alluded to in the archives were one and the same, there is additional reason for placing the columned building in this part of the garden. 1. In 1788 it is stated that rocks were placed at intervals on a path leading from 'la ruine' to the '2 ième source du ravin' beyond the wooden bridge.⁵ Desjardins considers one of the 'sources' to have been close to the *poulaillers* which was at our right hand; this might have been the second spring.⁶ 2. Mique states that in 1780 he designed the model for a small architectural 'ruine' above the grotto.⁷ A note in the archives, dated 1777, speaks of the 'porte d'entrée au bout du grotte'.⁸ If, as we believe, we had

¹ These two paragraphs were added in the 1924 ed.

² [Another paper in the archives gives the relative cost of three buildings: 'Ruine', 9358 livres; Temple de l'Amour, 41,593 livres; Belvédère, 64,990 livres, 9 sous, 8 deniers. See Lescure, *Les Palais de Trianon*, p. 107. Note added in 1924 ed.]

³ [The Temple de l'Amour is more than once called a 'ruine'. Another, near the 'Onze Arpents', had six Corinthian pillars. Note added in 1924 ed.]

⁴ *Arch. Nat.* O¹, 1878.   ⁵ *Ibid.*, O¹, 1882.   ⁶ Desjardins, p. 90.

⁷ ['5th Dec. 1780, Commencé par ordre de M. Mique le modèle de la partie de la grotte . . . du côté des montagnes . . . là dessus une petite ruine d'architecture l'avoir penté, planté, et gazonné.' Note added in 1924 ed.]

⁸ *Arch. Nat.* O¹, 1875.

5. THE ROCHER BRIDGE, WITH THE
BELVÉDÈRE BEYOND, 1952

6. THE LOGES DU CORPS DE GARDE. 1952

just passed out of the gardener's yard by this 'porte d'entrée', we should have been close to the earliest placed grotto.

In 1909 two old maps were procured from Paris; in one, dated 1840 (?), there is something which may indicate a small round building placed on the *rocher* behind the Belvédère. The other map was reproduced from an old one of 1705, but added to until a railway appears in it. In this map below the name 'pavillon de musique' (the Belvédère) is the name 'Le Kiosque'. It does not seem likely that a second name for the Belvédère should be given, and it may therefore refer to something else which does not appear in this map. Therefore the mere chance name which from the first moment we gave to our building was justified by there having been something called by that name exactly in that part of the garden.

In 1910 we looked out this name in the best etymological French dictionary and found that it was admitted to the French Academy in 1762 as 'pavillon ouvert de tous côtés': and defined by Thévenot (contemporary) as 'kioch ou divan qui est maintenu de huit grosses colonnes'.

THE MAN BY THE KIOSK

On our first visit a dark-complexioned man, marked by smallpox, was sitting close to the kiosk; he wore a large dark cloak and a slouch hat.

Though we were assured in 1908 by a very good authority that no gentleman now living at Versailles would wear a large cloak either in winter or summer, there might be nothing surprising in what we saw if the kiosk could be found. But considering that it is gone, it is historically interesting that we discovered in 1904 that there is one man in the story of Trianon who exactly suits the description.

Most of the intimate accounts of the period say that the comte de Vaudreuil was a Creole and marked by smallpox.[1] He was at

[1] A. M. P. G. de Nolhac, *La Reine Marie Antoinette*, 1898, pp. 61, 212.

one time one of the Queen's innermost circle of friends, but acted an enemy's part in persuading her to gain the King's permission for the acting of the politically dangerous play of *Le Mariage de Figaro*. The King had long refused to allow it, saying that it would cause the Bastille to be taken. The earlier play by the same author, *Le Barbier de Séville*,[1] was acted at Trianon on 13th September 1784, and also on 19th August 1785, just at the beginning of the diamond necklace episode, when Vaudreuil took the part of Almaviva and was dressed for it in a large dark cloak and Spanish hat.

In 1908 we found out from Madame Éloffe's *Journal* (the Queen's modiste) that in 1789 the broad-brimmed hat had entirely displaced the three-cornered hat, and was fashionable; also that swords were no longer generally worn.[2]

Vaudreuil left the Court of France among the first party of *émigrés* after the taking of the Bastille, July 1789.

THE RUNNING MAN

Though we were surprised when the second man, also dressed in a large cloak and hat, ran up to us, and with extreme earnestness directed us to go to the right rather than to the left, yet we merely thought his manner very French; and as he said, in the course of a rather long, unintelligible sentence, 'cherchez la maison,' we imagined that he understood that we were looking for the house, and followed his direction. We noticed that he

---

[1] *Le Barbier de Séville*, by Beaumarchais, was first played in 1775. A second play bringing in the same characters, *Le Mariage de Figaro*, was acted in 1781 at Vaudreuil's private theatre at Gennevilliers and at the Odéon, 1783, and for the first time in Paris, by permission, 27th April, 1784.

[2] 'Le chapeau rond à larges bords, que l'on appelait à la jockey, remplaçait déjà le chapeau à trois cornes nommé à l'Androsmane. On avait quitté le rabat, la bourse, les manchettes et l'épée.'—Comte de Reiset, *Modes et Usages, Livre Journal de Madame Éloffe*, 1885, vol. i., p. 479. [Quotation added in 1924 ed.]

[In June 1911 an engraving was sent to us of the slouch hat and cloak used in the Italian opera in France (*Barbiere di Seviglia*), which became for a few years in France the height of fashion. Added in 1924 ed.]

stood in front of a rock and seemed to come 'either over, round, or through it'.

The following year (1902) we learned that there was a tradition that on 5th October 1789 a messenger was sent to Trianon to warn the Queen of the approach of the mob from Paris: that she wished to walk back to the Palace by the most direct route, but the messenger begged her to wait at the house whilst he fetched the carriage, as it was safer to drive back as usual by the broad roads of the park.

A local tradition affirming this has been embodied by Madame Julie Lavergne in a volume entitled *Légendes de Trianon*. This particular scene in the story, called 'La Dernière Rose', interested us greatly, for it seemed to come from an eye-witness, and recalled many of the points of our vision. The Queen, it is said, had been walking with and talking to Marion (the daughter of an under-gardener) before going to her favourite grotto. After remaining there some time, and on growing alarmed at her own sad thoughts, the Queen called to Marion and was surprised to see, instead of the girl, a 'garçon de la Chambre' suddenly appear, trembling in all his limbs. After reading the letter brought to her from the Minister at the Palace, the Queen desired him to order the carriage and to let Madame de Tourzel know. The messenger bowed (as our man had done) and, once out of sight, ran off at full speed. The Queen followed him to the house.[1]

Enquiries through the publisher, in 1907, as to Madame Lavergne's sources of information, elicited the fact that her informant as to every detail of that scene had been Marion herself. This Marion, the *Légendes* tell us, afterwards married M. Charpentier, an under-gardener, known in 1789 by the name of 'Jean de l'Eau', on account of his bringing water daily from Ville d'Avray for the Queen's table.[2] He afterwards became *jardinier*

[1] *Légendes de Trianon*, p. 75.
[2] Lavergne, 'La Belle Jardinière', [in *Légendes de Trianon*], pp. 91, 97.

en chef, being appointed in 1805 by Napoleon in succession to Antoine Richard.[1]

The name 'Charpantier' appears in 1786 amongst the 'ouvriers terrassiers', who clear up sticks and leaves, plant flowers, and rake the ground.[2]

In 1783 'Mariamne' received wages for picking up leaves in the Trianon grounds;[3] this is quite possible, as children are said to have been used for that work, and the absence of surname suggests that she was the daughter of one of the gardeners.

The marriage certificate of Alexandre Charpentier, in 1823, gives his father's name as Louis Toussaint Charpentier, and his mother's name as Marie Anne Lemaignan. The marriage certificate of these older persons (from which we should have learnt their age) is said to have been destroyed.[4]

In the wages-book the names of two 'Lemonguin' (elder and younger) appear; also 'Magny', but not, so far as has been discovered, Lemaignan.[5] If this Marie Anne Charpentier was twenty-one years old at her son's birth (November 1796), she would have been eight years old in 1783, and fourteen in 1789. This would suit the 'Mariamne' of the archives, Madame Lavergne's story, and the girl seen by Miss Jourdain.

Two more points show the faithfulness of 'Marion's' account of that scene. Madame Lavergne (quoting her) says that 'pale rays of autumn sunshine lighted up the faded flowers'. It must, therefore, have been fairly fine; and in the wages-book it appears that on 5th October 1789 all the gardeners were at work *in the grounds*,

[1] [Claude Richard was appointed *jardinier en chef* at Trianon, 1750. He was the intimate friend of Linnæus, who called him the 'cleverest gardener in Europe'. He was the son of François Richard, who followed James II from Windsor to St. Germains. The son of Claude was Antoine Richard, who became *jardinier-botaniste-adjoint* at Trianon, 1765, *jardinier en chef*, 1784–1805, and died 1807. Desjardins, pp. 10–22. Note added in 1924 ed.]

[2] *Arch. Nat.* O[1], 1878.　　　　　[3] *Ibid.*, 1877.

[4] Letter enclosing marriage certificate (copy from the Archives Municipales, Versailles).

[5] *Arch. Nat.* O[1], 1876, 1877: [old lists of undergardeners at the Petit Trianon. Added in 1924 ed.]

and it is stated that on wet days they worked under cover, sometimes clearing out the passages of the house.[1] Secondly, she says
that the Queen sat at the entrance of her grotto, where fallen
leaves choked the course of the 'ruisseau'. From entries of pay-
ment it appears that the streams were cleared of dead leaves on
1st, 2nd and 3rd October 1789, but not on the 4th or 5th, or ever
again.[2] It is exactly a point which Marion would have noticed.

Madame Lavergne lived at Versailles from 1838 till her marriage in 1844, at which time Marion would have been sixty-
nine; and as Alexandre Charpentier was head-gardener at the
Petit Trianon for over fifty years, his mother would have been
easily accessible to Madame Lavergne, during her repeated visits
to Trianon, even after her marriage. Her father, M. Georges
Ozanneaux, was a personal friend of Louis Philippe, and was constantly about in the royal palaces.[3]

It is necessary to speak of the grotto; for Madame Campan says
that the Queen 'était assise dans sa grotte . . . lorsqu'elle reçut
un mot d'écrit . . . qui la suppliait de rentrer à Versailles'.[4]
Madame Lavergne says 'Marion se dirigea vers le parterre des
rosiers, et la Reine alla s'asseoir à l'entrée de sa grotte favorite,
auprès de la petite source. Les feuilles jaunies tombées des arbres
couvraient la terre et obstruaient le cours du ruisseau. . . . Le
murmure de la petite cascade qui arrose l'intérieur de la grotte,
retentissait seul dans le bosquet. . . . Effrayée d'être seule, elle
appela Marion; mais, au lieu de la jeune fille, un garçon de la
Chambre . . . parut, une lettre à la main.'[5] The Queen cannot,
therefore, have been many steps away from the grotto, at one
end or the other, when the messenger came to her.

---

[1] *Ibid.* O¹, 1879. [It was a wet morning in Paris, but the rain did not
begin at Versailles till 4 p.m. (*Mercure de Paris*). By the evening it was
heavy, and this helped to clear the mob away from the Place d'Armes
during the first part of the night. Added in 1924 ed.]
[2] *Ibid.* O¹, 1879.
[3] Lavergne, *Vie de Madame Lavergne.*
[4] Quoted in Lescure, p. 148.
[5] *Légendes de Trianon*, p. 75.

An Adventure

In 1904 we asked to be shown this grotto, and we were taken one on the farther side of the Belvédère, near the hill called l'Escargot, which was formed in 1781. We felt sure that this could not have been either of the two grottos spoken of in the archives.

In 1777 the end of one grotto is mentioned as being near the *porte d'entrée*, 'à la cloison de la porte d'entrée du jardin au bout du grotte trois pottereaux et deux traverses'.[1]

In 1777 there was a 'projet d'un pont et chutte en rocher, avec parapet'. This was probably a bridge (the Vergelay bridge?) over the principal river where it issued from the larger lake. The river was made at this time.[2]

In June, 1780, a new 'petite rivière' was planned to receive the water drained from the 'ravin de la grotte', and to conduct it into the larger lake. For this purpose a new grotto was made of a 'forme ovale, ornée en glaçon', through which the 'petite rivière' was to run.[3] A 'ravin du petit pont' was also planned.[4]

In August, 1780, masses of rock were procured, and the 'petite rivière' was begun and also a hill was thrown up 'pour couvrir la grotte'.[5]

In September, 1780, 'Bourdin a passé la journée . . . à poser le deuxième pont venant du côté de la grotte.'[6] This second bridge was probably the present Rocher bridge, being the second placed over the lakes. Neither of these two bridges would be the 'pont de bois',[7] and 'la conduitte en bois',[8] two descriptions of, and identical with, the one alluded to in the words 'ravin du petit pont', which was said to have been erected on high ground 'au dessus de Rocher du Ravin'.[9]

In December, 1780, the work was finished: 'Conduitte de

---

[1] *Arch. Nat.* O¹, 1875.　　　　[2] *Ibid.*
[3] This was the Queen's grotto.
[4] *Arch. Nat.* O¹, 1875.　　[5] *Ibid.*　　　[6] *Ibid.*
[7] *Arch. Nat.* O¹, 1882. (There was also a 'pont de bois à la porte verte' on the east side of the house.—*Arch. Nat.* O¹, 1881 and 1882.)
[8] *Ibid.*　　　　[9] *Ibid.*, Hezecques, p. 242.

l'exécution de la grotte, petite rivière, et chutte d'eau retombante dans le grand lac, autres petits ravins dans la montagne près du grand lac à la fin de la petite rivière de la grotte.'[1]

In 1781 a 'montagne' was made 'en face du jardin français—en face de la comédie'.[2]

In March and April, 1781, a hill called 'l'Escargot' was piled up[3]—beyond the Belvédère—and, presumably, a third and very small grotto was made. The creation of the 'Escargot' hill would have made the 'ravin' on the north side of the Belvédère, which is still visible, and leads to the greater lake.

There are several reasons why we think that the Queen's grotto (the second made) was on the theatre side of the Belvédère:

1. D'Hezecques's description of it in 1789 shows that, though a 'ruisseau' passed through it, persons could go freely out at both ends;[4] whereas when water was passing down through the upper entrance of the 'escargot' grotto, no one could have used it at the same time: there is only room for the water.

2. He speaks of the 'prairie' being visible from 'une crevasse, qui s'ouvrait à la tête du lit'; this would have been possible from a grotto on the theatre side, but not on the other, as the 'Escargot' hill would have been in the way.

3. D'Hezecques describes a staircase which 'conduisait au sommet de la roche', enabling persons to leave hurriedly. There is something like an ancient rock staircase attached to the back of the large rock, giving the name to the Rocher bridge.

4. He says that the grotto was very dark on first entering, and L'Espinasse's picture of the Belvédère in 1783 shows the opening to a cavern on its southern side close to the Rocher bridge,[5] which could be truly described as 'venant du côté de la grotte'. Could the rock out of which the cavernous mouth was cut have been lifted over the long bridge at some later time? for in L'Espinasse's

[1] *Ibid.*, 1877.   [2] *Ibid.*
[3] *Arch. Nat. O¹*, 1877.   [4] Hezecques, p. 243, 244.
[5] Desjardins, picture, p. 196.

picture there is no such rock over the Rocher bridge as there is now, and the cavern has disappeared.

5. The map of 1783 represents (according to Desjardins) 'le projet de Mique complètement exécuté'. In it the figure (5) (indicating the grotto) occurs both at the 'Escargot' and also on the theatre side of the Belvédère.

In September, 1910, Miss Jourdain was asked whether she had seen a map recently placed in the front hall of the Petit Trianon, and she said she had not. On going there she found the map, which had not been there at any of her former visits, and saw that the grottos were put, as far as she could judge, just where we had long ago, through elaborate personal research, decided must be their real position. She could only make this out by standing on the table amongst the books and photographs, the map being hung too high to be easily seen.[1]

Several further points of interest have emerged in connection with the running man.

1. In April, 1908, we learned that our being directed at all in the grounds was unusual, for since September, 1870, they have been thrown open until dark. The difficulty now experienced is to find a guide.

2. He spoke of the 'maison'. In 1907 we found out that the Queen was in the habit of calling the Petit Trianon 'ma maison de Trianon', to distinguish it from the Palace and the Château.[2] Louis XVI had presented it to Marie Antoinette on his accession.

3. The Queen is reported by Marion to have addressed the messenger as 'Breton'.[3] This was not an uncommon name about the Court and old Versailles. The Court almanac for 1783 shows that then the Queen had a Page 'de l'Écurie', called 'de

[1] [Since 1911 le Guide Joanne has called the Rocher bridge 'le pont de bois sur une ravine . . . on remonte à son extrémité le petit ruisseau qui l'alimente et on gagne un second petit lac.' The bridge we passed over was on high ground out of sight of the lake; the little cascade and the *petite rivière*, both of which passed through the Queen's grotto, have disappeared with it. Note added in 1924 ed.]

[2] Desjardins, pp. 73, 103.   [3] *Légendes de Trianon*, p. 75.

Results of Research

Bretagne'. (The Pages de la Chambre sometimes became 'de l'Écurie' before receiving a commission or some other office.[1]) He is not mentioned in the almanac of 1789, but (as we know from other instances) it does not follow necessarily that he had no office in the household. Madame Éloffe (the Queen's modiste) mentions a Mademoiselle Breton amongst the Queen's women, who does not appear in the almanac.[2]

If 'de Bretagne' was sixteen years old in 1783, he would have been twenty-two in 1789—just in the fresh young vigour suitable to our running man.

The name 'Breton' may have referred to his nationality only, for in November, 1907, we discovered that the accent in which the man spoke to us resembled the Breton accent, in which the consonants are strengthened and the diphthongs broadened.

In the autumn of 1909 we read the Baron de Frénilly's *Souvenirs*, in which it is stated that wigs were universally worn by gentlemen in French society up till 1787. After that date powdered hair became the general usage; the first person (M. de Valence) who ventured to appear with unpowdered hair did so, apparently, in 1788, after which it became a mark of extreme fashion.[3]

The same was the case with buckled shoes. Gold, silver, stones and rosettes had been required for a gentleman's dress ornaments; but after the commercial treaty with England in 1786, steel was used for everything. Buckled shoes are expressly mentioned as being very fashionable in 1789, and there was, at that time, a rage for steel ornaments.[4]

BRIDGE OVER LITTLE CASCADE

Following the man's direction, we turned to the right and walked over a small rustic bridge which crossed a tiny waterfall coming from above us, on our right hand, and flowing in front of

[1] Hezceques, pp. 112, 118.
[2] Reiset, *Modes et Usages*, vol. i, p. 445.
[3] *Souvenirs du Baron de Frénilly*, 1908, p. 80.
[4] *Ibid.*

a little rocky cliff with ferns growing in the crevices. The water seemed to have formed a steep narrow little ravine, which shelved away below us to a little glimmering pool.

Neither bridge, nor cascade, nor ravine can be found, or anything suggesting them. In 1905 the person in charge at the house assured Miss Jourdain that there never had been more than one cascade, meaning the rush of water under the Rocher bridge. The Rocher bridge is certainly not the one we crossed, which was high above the level of the lakes.

In 1907 we bought *Souvenirs d'un Page* by the comte d'Hezecques. He says: 'En face du château, une pelouse . . . se terminait par une roche ombragée de pins, de thuyas, de mélèzes, et *surmontée d'un pont rustique*, comme on en rencontre dans les montagnes de la Suisse et les précipices du Valais. Cette perspective agreste et sauvage rendait plus douce celle . . . de la troisième façade du château.'[1]

He also speaks of water passing through the moss-lined grotto, which, according to our idea, must have been below us, but close by on our right hand.[2] Madame Lavergne writes of the 'petite cascade' and of the sound of it in the grotto.[3]

In April, 1908, extracts from Mique's accounts and plans for the Trianon grounds were procured from the archives, giving the history of the grottos: 'Juin 4, 1780, fait un modèle en terre *du ravin du petit pont*.'[4] '1788, Pièce au dessus du *Rocher du Ravin* et . . . passage des voitures sur *le pont de bois* . . . Pièce à droite *en face du Rocher du Ravin*.'[5] 'Au long du chemin de l'emplacement de la Ruine *sur la conduitte en bois à la deuxième source du Ravin*.'[6] The first source was probably close to the 'Ruine' (our kiosk?). The second 'source' might coincide with Desjardins' 'source', which he places a few steps from the *poulaillers*,[6] and was probably meant to feed the 'petite rivière',

---

[1] Hezecques, p. 242. [2] *Ibid.*, p. 243.
[3] La Dernière Rose, p. 75. [4] *Arch. Nat.* O¹, 1875.
[5] *Ibid.* O¹, 1882. [6] *Le Petit Trianon*, p. 90.

which passed through the Queen's grotto, carrying off the water from the stagnant pool between the grottos to the larger lake.[1] That would exactly agree with the position of our little cascade, small bridge, and glimmering pool.

In April, 1908, an old MS. map was found amongst such archive papers as relate to the grottos, showing a small bridge in the right position relatively to the lakes, the Rocher bridge, and the place where we believe the Queen's grotto to have been.

THE ISOLATED ROCK

In 1908 we found a mass of rocks standing in the dry bed of the small lake. On one rock covered with ivy were two full-grown pine-trees. It seems unlikely that the trees should have originally been in the small circular basin of water.

D'Hezecques says that thuya and pine-trees were planted high up over the grotto to give it the appearance of a Swiss mountain.[2] The grotto was destroyed about 1792, and it is possible that some of the rocks covering it were displaced and allowed to slip into the lake below, and that the present pine-trees may have been seedlings at the time, for we are told that the life of a pine-tree is from one hundred to two hundred years old.

In 1908 we noticed that at one side of this ivy-covered rock were peculiar projections; one of these was broken off short, but the other was intact. We thought they might once have formed supports for a small bridge.

Rocks are said to have been placed in 1788 at the 'montagne des Pins à gauche et en montant au Rocher', 'Montagne des Pins à droite en montant au Rocher.'[3]

In January, 1791, trees were torn up from the *montagnes*.

In February, March, April, 1792, every few days occurs the entry: 'Journée à arracher les Thuja sur les montagnes.'[4]

According to the old picture by L'Espinasse (1793), there was

[1] *Arch. Nat.* O¹, 1875. [2] d'Hezecques, p. 242.
[3] *Arch. Nat.* O¹, 1882. [4] *Ibid.* O¹, 1879.

nothing over the low long bridge between the two lakes, but there was by the side of it, just where the grotto would have ended, a cavern in a rock.[1] This is no longer there; but possibly the face of rock with the cavern-like opening may have been lifted over the bridge, and account for the very peculiar rock which is at present above the bridge, causing it to be called the Rocher bridge. A rough rock staircase which has no meaning is attached to this rock behind. D'Hezecques speaks of a staircase as having been within the grotto leading up to its entrance on the high ground on the *montagnes*—has it been moved to the lower end of the grotto?

There is now no isolated rock standing up as we saw it behind the running man—only mounds covered with shrubs and trees. But in the archives there is a note saying that in 1788 rocks were placed in various parts, and one is especially mentioned, 'pièce donnant au bord du lac de l'ancien côté des rochers . . . *au long du chemin de l'emplacement de la Ruine sur la conduitte en bois à la deuxième source du Ravin.*'[2] This would have been the path we were on in 1901.

PELOUSE

It is easy to suppose that between the years 1901–1904 trees were cleared away from the rough ground on the north side of the house, which in 1901 had given it the look of an orchard. So much was this the case that the lady sitting under the north terrace was thought to be making a study of tree stems; for she was looking into trees, and she held a large paper in her hand, and, as we passed, held it out at arm's-length.

At present there are trees on each side of the *pelouse*, and one growing near the site of the old Jeu de Bague, but none in front of the house, and it all looks drier, brighter, and less confined than in 1901.

We have found two interesting mentions of this *pelouse*.

[1] Desjardins, p. 196.   [2] *Arch. Nat.* O¹, 1882.

Results of Research

Before the new theatre was built in 1779 the old Comédie stood on it for three years. When the Comédie was removed it gave place to a 'pelouse parsemée d'arbres'.[1]

THE LADY

Nothing unusual marked the lady sitting on a low seat on the grass immediately under the north terrace. I remember recognising that her light-coloured skirt, white fichu, and straw hat were in the present fashion, but they struck me as rather dowdy in the general effect. She was so near us that I looked full at her, and she bent slightly forward to do the same.

I never doubted that we had both seen her, and three months after was astonished to hear that Miss Jourdain had not done so. That sounds simple to others, to ourselves it is inexplicable. Miss Jourdain had seen the plough, the cottage, the woman, and the girl, which I had not; but she is generally more observant than I, and there were other things to look at. At this moment there was nothing to see on the right, and merely a shady, damp-looking meadow on the left, and the lady was sitting in front of the house we had come to see, and were both eagerly studying. The lady was visible some way off. We walked side by side straight up to her, leaving her slightly on the left hand as we passed up the steps to the terrace, from whence I saw her again from behind, and noticed that her fichu had become a pale green.

The fact that she had not been seen at a moment when we were both a little exercised by our meeting with the men—one looking so unpleasant, and the other so unaccountably and infectiously excited—made a deep impression.

In the following winter we heard the legend of the Queen having been occasionally seen sitting in front of the house in the English garden, but of this we have no further proof. Three things, however, were to us full of interest:

[1] Desjardins, pp. 107, 120; *Arch. Nat.* O^1, 1875, 1877; E. Terrade, *Le Théâtre de la Reine*, 1885, p. 23.

71

An Adventure

1. In 1920 I saw Wertmüller's picture of the Queen, which alone of all the many portraits shown me in any way brought back the face I had seen; for the face was more square and the nose shorter. A few weeks later we read that Madame Campan considered it almost the only picture of her that was really like, though other people thought that it did not do her justice.

2. In April, 1908, we learned that there was only one time during the Queen's tenure of the Petit Trianon when she could have seen strangers in her gardens, from which, in earlier days, the Court was entirely excluded, and to which even the King only came by invitation. For four months, after May, 1789, until the Court was carried off to Paris, the public streamed in as it liked. So many came to see the place that had been too much talked about, that the King and Queen had gone that summer to Marly for a little rest and quiet. That was the time when d'Hezecques, with one of the deputies, walked round and saw the grotto and the little bridge. At the time, the Trianon officials must have learned to treat strangers with cold politeness, but probably resenting the necessity. This exactly accounts for the manner of the guards at the *porte du jardinier*; they made no difficulty, and told us that we should find the house by going that way, but they spoke in quite an unusual manner. It was mechanical and disengaged.

3. In the summer of 1908 we read the *Journal* of Madame Éloffe (the Queen's modiste). She says that during the year 1789 the Queen was extremely economical, and had very few dresses made. Madame Éloffe repaired several light, washing, short skirts, and made, in July and September, two green silk bodices, besides many large white fichus.[1] This agrees exactly with the dress seen in 1901. The skirt was not of a fresh white, but was light coloured—slightly yellowish. The white fichu in front seemed to have an edge of green or gold, just as it would have appeared if the white muslin, or gauze, was over green. The

[1] [Reiset, pp. 365, 369, 404, 423. Note added in 1924 ed.]

colour would have shown more clearly at the back, but in front,
where the white folds accumulated, the green would have been
less prominent. The straight edge in front and the frill behind
had often puzzled me, but in Madame Éloffe's illustrations of the
fashions at that time there are instances of the same thing.
There is in the book a coloured picture of the green silk bodice,
with all the measurements, to enable her to fit the Queen perfectly.[1]

JEU DE BAGUE

As we approached the terrace at the north-west corner of the
house we had some barrier on our right hand entirely blocking
the view, so that we could see nothing but the meadow on our
left hand, and the house with its terrace in front.

At present the pathway which curves towards the house, and
is very likely the old one, has a large bare space on the right hand
with one beautiful old tree growing on the edge of it; and from
some way off one can easily see across it to the chapel beyond the
French garden. A long piece of wall extends westward from the
terrace, round which one has to go into the French garden in
order to find the staircase; whilst the whole length of wall, including part of the north terrace, is hidden by a large old spread-
ing bush, completely covering the place where the lady sat.

Originally, we could not see the steps whilst on the path, but
after we had passed the barrier on our right hand we found them
at once without going round any wall.

The map of 1783[2] shows us that the Jeu de Bague (put up in
1776) once stood on what is now bare space. It was a circular
building surrounded by a wooden gallery, masked by trees. This
would have completely shut out the view, and the path was probably curved on its account.

In 1907 we learned that the Queen had a passage made under

[1] Reiset, *Modes et Usages*, vol. i, pp. 365, 369, 404, 423, 479.
[2] [By Contant de la Motte. Note added in 1924 ed.]

the terrace from the house to the Jeu de Bague; and in 1908 we discovered the old walled-up doorway leading into the English garden behind the bush. The ground seems to have been a good deal raised since it was used. Four feet to the right of this door, just at the point where the top of the present staircase is reached, is a change of masonry, the rest of the wall being plastered over.

In 1910 we found that this extension of the wall was composed of rubble. Perhaps it had been added to the stone terrace in the time of Louis Philippe. If the present staircase is old, we could have reached it easily from the English garden in the absence of the wall, but if it is not old—and it is not indicated in Mique's map—there may have been something quite different—even steps turned northward towards the English garden.

In 1910 we also learned that the bush had been planted when the duchesse d'Orléans occupied the house.[1]

THE CHAPEL MAN

Whilst we were standing at the south-west end of the terrace above the French garden, the door of a building at right angles to the house suddenly opened, and a young man came out and slammed the door behind him. He came to us very quickly along a level. His manner was jaunty and imperious, and he told us that the only way to the house was by the *cour d'honneur*. It was difficult to hear what he said. We thought at once that we were trespassing and looked for some way down from the terrace, upon which he constituted himself our guide, and with an inquisitive, amused expression went with us a little way down the French garden, and showed us out into the avenue by a broad road.

There is much to say about this incident.

1. The man evidently did not mean us to stand on the terrace so near to the house, and forced us to move away. He was the second person that afternoon who had excitedly insisted on our

[1] [The bush which is shown in photographs was cleared away in 1921. Note added in 1924 ed.]

going one way rather than another; but now we know that since 1870 the gardens and terraces have been made public until dark, and people walk about freely. No one has ever stopped us since, nor can we hear of anyone else who has been guided as we were.

2. In 1905 we found that the building out of which the man came was the old chapel, which is in a ruinous condition.

In 1906 Miss Jourdain had leave to go into the chapel, which she had to enter from the avenue, there being no entrance from the garden. When inside she saw that the door out of which he had come was one leading into the royal gallery. The gallery now stands isolated high up on the north wall of the chapel. Formerly, from inside, it was reached by a door on a landing at the top of a staircase. This staircase is completely broken down, and the floor of the landing is gone, so that there is now no access to the gallery or to the second door opening on to the terrace. Both doors are bolted, barred, and cob-webbed over from age and disuse. The guide said that the doors had not been opened in the memory of any man there, not since it was used by the Court.

In April, 1907, Miss Jourdain went again to the chapel, this time with two companions. Their guide then told them that the doors had not been opened, to his knowledge, for fifteen years, and the great door not since it was used by the Court of Louis XVI. 'Moi, je suis ici depuis quinze ans, et je sais que les portes ont été condamnées bien avant cela.' He added that, having the sole charge of the keys, no one could have opened the doors without his knowledge, and smiled at the idea as he looked at the blocked-up old doors.

In August, 1907, two other friends went to the chapel and entirely confirmed all that had been said about its ruined condition and the impossibility of the great door having been opened in 1901. Their guide told them that the big door had been Marie Antoinette's private entrance. The gallery was still standing, and had two chairs of gilt and old red velvet on it; but when they asked whether it was possible to enter it, the guide laughed and pointed to the staircase. There was no other entrance, he said, and the stairs had been in that condition for the last ten years. They thought from the look of the stairs that they had probably been so for much longer.

In September, 1910, a fifth friend went to the chapel and bore witness to the impossibility of the doors having been used in 1901, and was told that the staircase had finally broken down fifteen years before.

3. From Desjardins' book we learned that the Queen's concierge had been Bonnefoy du Plan. He had rooms between the chapel and the *cour d'honneur*, and kept his stores in a loft over the chapel, reached by the now broken-down old staircase. The window of this attic looks over the terraces, and from it he would have seen anyone approaching the house from that side. The name of the *suisse* (the porter) in charge of the *porte du perron de la chapelle* in 1789 was Lagrange. His rooms were immediately behind the chapel, looking into the avenue.[1] He could easily have been sent through the chapel to interview strangers on the terrace.

4. We did not lose sight of the man when he came to us. As it is now he must have gone quite out of sight, down one flight of steps outside the chapel door, and (after passing under a high wall) have reached the terrace (where we were standing) by a second set of steps. The present wall of the chapel courtyard is so high as to hide half the door, and a large chestnut-tree in the courtyard hides it from the part of the terrace on which we were —even in winter.

In April, 1907, we discovered that a continuous groundfloor passage from the kitchens once passed the chapel to the house. This set us wondering as to whether there had ever been a pathway above it. The same year we were told that the chapel courtyard round which the passage had gone had been enlarged.

In August, 1907, two friends reported to us and photographed

[1] Desjardins, pp. 188, 189.

a mark on the outside of the courtyard wall brought out by the damp, showing where it might at some time have been raised.

In March, 1908, another mark on the chapel was discovered, revealing that there had once been an inner wall to the courtyard, which might have been removed when the courtyard was enlarged. We also found out that the levels were so different that the passage would have been partly underground on the side of the French garden, but not so in the *rez-de-chaussée* in the courtyard and where it flanked the *cour d'honneur*. We noticed from the photographs that the bastion at the south-west corner of the house in the *cour d'honneur* looked older than the top part of the wall adjoining it above the chapel courtyard.

In September, 1910, permission was given to enter this courtyard: when within, it was definitely explained that above the kitchen passage there had been a covered way, by which the Queen could enter the chapel from the house in wet weather. The top of this covered way had been *de plain pied*, joining the bit of terrace outside the chapel door to the terrace by the house. This would have been the level way along which our man came to us.

The marks of the passage and covered way (forming the intervening piece of terrace) were perfectly clear both on the inside of the present wall and on the ground in the courtyard. The present balustrade adjoining the bastion was probably placed when the old covered way was destroyed and the outside wall was raised. It was also noticed that the round windows in the bastion lighted the lower kitchen passage, but that those facing the French garden, being on a higher level, lighted the covered way.

The guide stated that the tree in the centre of the chapel courtyard had certainly been planted after the days of the monarchy.

5. The road from the garden to the avenue (through which

An Adventure

the man ushered us) was not far from the chapel, and was broad enough to admit a coach. The present one is narrower and farther to the west.

In 1907 we read a note by M. de Nolhac in *Les Consignes de Marie Antoinette* in which he said that the old *porte de la ménagerie*, which must have led from the avenue to the French garden, is now lost, but that it must have been 'tout auprès des bâtiments de la Conciergerie et des cuisines'.[1] We thought that perhaps it was the one we went by, and on looking at Mique's map of 1783[2] found a broad road dividing the kitchen court into two parts. At present solid continuous buildings on the two sides of the kitchen court show no sign of an entrance, though in two places the roofs have a difference of level.

In April, 1909, a Frenchman, who sold prints and seemed to be a specialist in maps, said that Mique's map was the only authoritative one.

In September, 1910, we learned from the first authority that Mique's map was 'exact': that the road found in it had certainly existed, and its position relatively to the pond in the French garden was explained. A search for some sign of it was at once made, and successfully. On the garden side, not at all far from the chapel, the jamb of an old opening still projects from the building, covered with ivy; and the stones on the ground are laid, for a space of about twelve paces, the other way from the stones on either side, evidently to make a carriage road. A large rectangular stone was lying on the ground, which might have been either a step or part of the second jamb. On the avenue side marks of an opening of some sort can be traced through the plaster with which Louis Philippe finished the buildings after restoring and also altering them. The opening would have included two present windows not far from the *porte de la bouche*, as the signs of it are visible on both sides of the opening, and the space between is from twelve to twenty paces.

[1] Page 7.   [2] Copied by Contant de la Motte.

78

Results of Research

Within the kitchen court the buildings have been so altered and plastered over that no traces of change could be found.

All these points correspond with our recollection of the roadway through which we had passed in 1901.

TWO LABOURERS WITH CART AND HORSE

On her second visit, 2nd January 1902, Miss Jourdain saw, in the field near the Hameau, two labourers, in brown tunics and bright coloured short capes, loading a cart with sticks. The capes hardly came below their shoulders and had hoods: one was bright blue and the other red.

In May, 1904, a search was made in the archives, with the result that it was clear that carts and horses for the purpose of tidying the grounds were hired by the day in old times, and not kept in the farm for constant use. In January, 1789, two men, instead of the usual one ('plus un homme'), were hired 'pour ramasser les loques des chenilles et les brûler'.[1]

In 1906 we discovered that the tunic and short cape were worn by the bourgeoisie in the fourteenth century.[2]

In April, 1908, we had proof that artisans were wearing them in the eighteenth century,[3] and that some of the working men at Trianon in 1776 had *hardes de couleur*.[4]

The entry in the wages-book showed that, up to 1783, from time to time 'une voiture à un cheval, et un conducteur', were hired for picking up branches and sticks in the parks; but on *4th October* 1789 a cart with two horses (almost certainly requiring two men) was hired *for three days* for the purpose.[5]

In August, 1908, a former gardener, who had been at Trianon

---

[1] *Arch. Nat.* O¹, 1879. [Caterpillars' nests were hacked out of the bark of trees, and these bits of wood were collected from the ground and carried away in a cart for burning. Note added in 1924 ed.]

[2] [See illustrations of the period. Note added in 1924 ed.]

[3] [*Les Foires des Rues de Paris*, Musée Carnavalet. Note added in 1924 ed.]

[4] *Arch. Nat.* O¹, 1877.   [5] *Arch. Nat.* O¹, 1879.

79

long enough to remember both the Charpentiers, father and son, laughed at the idea of such a dress being worn now at Trianon, as it belonged to the *ancien régime*. He assured us that carts of the present day in France had scarcely altered at all in type, and that the two now in use at Trianon (which we found in a shed at the *ferme*) were of the old pattern.

THE WOOD

Miss Jourdain then went from the Hameau towards the small Orangerie. Whilst on the ascending path she saw, on looking back, a man passing in front of, or in, a distant plantation on his way to the Hameau. He was dressed in a cloak and hat of the pattern that we had seen the previous summer.

She then descended to the low ground in front of the Belvédère and crossed one of the bridges over the principal river (not the Rocher bridge, but possibly the Vergelay bridge). After going forward a little she turned, meaning to go back to the Hameau, and recrossed either the same bridge or the next one, which is very near the Vergelay. She immediately found herself in a wood of very tall trees, with such high thick undergrowth that (even though it was winter) she could not see through it. Well-kept paths opened at intervals right and left at different angles, and they gave the impression of being so arranged as to lead round and round. She had the feeling of being in the midst of crowds passing and repassing her and heard voices and sounds of dresses. On looking back she found the view as completely blocked as it was in front and to the sides. After vainly pursuing the confusing paths for some time she found herself close to the hill leading to the Orangerie.

In 1904 and in 1908 we tried to find this wood, without result. There are open plantations, but they have no undergrowths concealing paths from one another, even in summer. Several people have gone independently to look for the wood, but have not found it.

Results of Research

In 1905 Miss Jourdain was told by the chief authority that in this direction trees had been thinned and not replaced.

The entries in the archives indicate that there must have been woods near by in which paths were cut for the Queen; it is also likely that the older woods, such as *Les Onze Arpents*, are not referred to; for when these plantations were made thousands of lower shrubs were bought to be placed under the trees, and these were paid for by the King.[1] In the gardener's wages-book the gathering up and occasional burnings of undergrowths in a wood (apparently in this part of the garden) are alluded to.[2]

In Mique's map (1783) the wood with its diverging paths, can be plainly seen.[3] It is approached by the two bridges over the river, and stretches towards the hill on which the Orangerie stands.

THE MUSIC

Whilst in the wood Miss Jourdain heard sounds of a stringed band drifting past her from the direction of the house. The sounds were very soft and intermittent. She could afterwards write down from memory about twelve bars, in the key of A flat, but without all the inner harmonies.

She ascertained immediately afterwards that no band had been playing out-of-doors that afternoon at Versailles. It was a cold, wet winter's afternoon.

In March, 1907, the twelve bars were shown to a musical expert, who said (without having heard the story) that the bars could hardly all belong to one another, but that the idiom dated from 1780. He found a grammatical mistake in one bar. After hearing the story, he suggested the name of Sacchini.

In March, 1908, Miss Jourdain and a friend were told in Versailles that no bands had been allowed to play in the park in winter until 1907. They also ascertained that no music played at Versailles, or in the park, could have been heard at Trianon.

[1] *Arch. Nat.* O¹, 1876.   [2] *Ibid.*, 1877.
[3] [Copied by Contant de la Motte. Note added in 1924 ed.]

An Adventure

In the same month they searched through a great deal of unpublished music in the Conservatoire de Musique at Paris, and discovered that the twelve bars represented the chief motives of the light opera of the eighteenth century, excluding Rameau and his school, and that, as far as they could discover, nothing like them occurred in the opera of 1815 onward. Such passages were found in Sacchini, Philidor, Monsigny, Grétry and Pergolesi. Grammatical mistakes were found in Monsigny and Grétry.

Sacchini.

'Dardanus.' General likeness.

'Œdipe à Colone.' Number 6. Two bars intact in the key of A natural answering to that heard in 1902, allowing for the rise of a semitone, which had taken place since the eighteenth century. (This was proved by later editions of operatic music, in which the songs were dropped a semitone to retain the original key.)

Philidor, in a collection of single airs (Rigaudons, 1767)—the cadence.

'Le Maréchal Ferrand': repetition of single notes, the first bar of the melody, and many other hints of likeness.

Duni. 1765. The same general characteristics, but no exact resemblance.

Monsigny.

'Le Roi et le Fermier.' Written for performance at the opening of the new theatre at the Petit Trianon, 1st August 1780, when the Queen first acted herself. Up to 1908 it had not been republished. In it the figure of the first of the twelve bars was found.

'Le Déserteur.' No published edition was found after 1830. In one published before that date the last three bars of the music were found, and the melody of the first bars was assigned to the second violins, and very freely, in inversions and variations, in other places. The character of the accompaniment was similar to that heard.

82

Grétry.

The same phrases were used and the ascending passage was found.

Pergolesi.

'Largo and Andante in D.' Similar phrases were used.

THE TALL GARDENER

Miss Jourdain then went along the upper path, and when between the Escargot hill and the Belvédère she met a very tall gardener of apparently great strength, with long muscular arms. She thought that with his long hair and grizzled, untidy beard and general appearance, he had the look of an Englishman rather than a Frenchman.

He was dressed in a rough knitted jersey, and a small dark blue round cap was set at the back of his head. She enquired where she should find the Queen's grotto, and he walked a little way beside her to show her the way.

Miss Jourdain expected to have to turn back to the present grotto, and when she remarked that they were going past the Belvédère, he replied firmly that they *must* go past the Belvédère, and said that it was necessary to have been born and bred in the place to know the way so that 'personne ne pourrait vous tromper'.

It appears that from 1870 onwards the gardeners at Trianon have been selected from the technical schools, and that it is now a matter of competition, no one being appointed simply because he was born and bred there. We do not know whether this is the case with the under-gardeners; nor whether the tall gardener was a chief official or not.

In August, 1908, we were told by a former gardener that their dress is now the same as the traditional dress of the *ancien régime* —viz. a rough knitted jersey, with a small *casquette* on the head.

In the old weekly wages-book there appears, for several years, the name 'l'Anglais'—probably a nickname.[1] He must not be confused with John Egleton, who remained at Trianon only a few months, and whose wages were settled on his departure by a bill which is still in existence, but is not in the wages-book.[2]

We owe our researches as to the position of the Queen's grotto almost entirely to the tall gardener's decided directions and guidance to the part of the English garden between the Belvédère and the *montagnes* close to the theatre.

[We found, some years later, that this position had been accepted as correct.

Many persons have stated in writing that they had heard and read the complete narratives of our first visit to the Petit Trianon before any historical investigations into the past conditions of the place had been made.][3]

C.A.E.M.

E.F.J.

September, 1910

[1] *Arch. Nat.* O¹, 1877. [2] *Ibid.*, 1880.
[3] The passage bracketed was added in the 1924 ed.

CHAPTER III

Answers to questions which we have been asked

1. One of us has to own to having powers of second sight, etc., deliberately undeveloped, and there are psychical gifts in her family. She comes of a Huguenot stock. The other is one of a large and cheerful party, being the seventh daughter and of a seventh son; her mother and grandmother were entirely Scotch, and both possessed powers of premonition accompanied by vision. Her family has always been sensitive to ghost stories in general, but mercilessly critical of particular ones of a certain type.

2. Both of us have inherited a horror of all forms of occultism. We lose no opportunity of preaching against them as unwholesome and misleading; because they mostly deal with conditions of physical excitement, and study of the abnormal and diseased, including problems of disintegrated personality which present such close analogy to those of insanity. We have the deepest distrust in, and distaste for, stories of abnormal appearances and conditions. We find narratives of *revenants* unconvincing, and studiously avoid (as utterly lowering) all spiritualistic methods of communication with the dead. We have never had the curiosity, or the desire, to help in the investigations of psychical phenomena.

3. We belong to no new schools of thought: we are the daughters of English clergymen, and heartily hold and teach the faith of our fathers.

4. We are quite certain that neither of us exerted any conscious influence over the other; for though we saw much in common, yet each had independent vision. We should think it wrong either to exercise, or to submit to, influence of that nature. We are independent people and accustomed to stand on our own feet.

5. Our condition at the time was one of perfect health and enjoyment of a holiday in the midst of very hard work.

6. We were entirely ignorant of the history and traditions of the place, and continued our conversation about other things after every interruption. We did not even know that we were in the grounds of the Petit Trianon until we saw the house.

7. At the time Miss Jourdain thought that there was something unusual about the place and was puzzled; the same idea returned to her occasionally during the following week. Miss Moberly put her feeling of oppression down to some physical fatigue in herself, and so said nothing; for we did not know one another very well at that time, were in the relation of hostess and guest, and neither of us thought of enlarging on uncomfortable sensations. After some days, when Miss Moberly was writing an account of the expedition, she thought it over with care, and realised that her sensations had not been caused by fatigue, but had produced fatigue. She became convinced that the oppression had been due to some unusual cause in the place itself, and instantly turned to Miss Jourdain and said so. Miss Jourdain agreed. We then discussed the man by the kiosk and the running man, but said that there was much besides which had caused dreamy depression. Miss Moberly returned to her letter and wrote down: 'We both think that the Petit Trianon is haunted.'

When we met next (three months later) we talked it over again, and finding that Miss Jourdain had not seen the lady, and that Miss Moberly had not seen the plough, cottage, woman, or girl, we resolved to write separate accounts of our visit in order to find the discrepancies, but with no idea of making exhaustive histories. These papers are still in existence. Miss Jourdain, in her story, used the words 'uncanny' and 'eerie' to describe her feelings, but they did not mean that she had the least idea at the time that any of the people encountered were unreal or ghostly; this was still more true of the scenery.

8. During the next three years, Miss Jourdain repeatedly took parties of girls over the Trianon, and she reported that the place was changed; but Miss Moberly could not believe it, and even made maps to remind her what their old route had been. After Miss Moberly had paid a second visit to Trianon in July, 1904, and had found out for herself that the place was entirely changed, it was resolved to undertake a personal research into the matter, and to say no more until we had discovered for ourselves whether our vivid recollections of the people and the place tallied with any ancient reality or not.

Up to that time we had told the story freely, with the result that we have constantly traced it inaccurately reported in histories, sometimes purporting to have come from other sources, and even in newspapers and small periodicals. After research had begun to yield interesting results, we were obliged to be silent, finding that publicity prevented our getting at evidence.

We were very busy people, and have refused to let the incident take a prominent place in our time, interests, or fancy, though from the first we agreed to lose no given opportunity of elucidation. The evidence has, therefore, come slowly; but the manner in which it has come has often been a source of surprise. If a helpful person came in our way, we showed the whole thing: if we were casually asked if certain reports were true, we confirmed them (when we could), but said nothing further. We were anxious to wait until we had exhausted every possible means of satisfying ourselves as to the exact amount of interest attaching to the story; and it was several years before we had to believe that we had seen the place as it had been a hundred years before, and as it had not been, in several important particulars, since 1835.

An Adventure

The research had been undertaken with the idea of *disproving* the suggestion that anything unusual had happened, for we were resolved not to deceive ourselves or anyone else, if personal industry could prevent it.

9. In the course of the last four or five years, Miss Jourdain has searched for evidence bearing on the story (either by word or picture) in the Archives nationales, in the library, museum, Mairie, and Archives départementales at Versailles: also in the libraries Nationale, Hôtel de Ville, and in the Musée Carnavalet, and in the Conservatoire de Musique at Paris. She has poked about in French book and print shops, and must have seen a large number of originals of the published plans, illustrations, and accounts of the place. We believe that there is not likely to be any striking documentary evidence other than we have dealt with.

10. The historical interest of the story seems to depend on the truth of the tradition that the Queen went to Trianon on October 5th, 1789. We can find no negative evidence of this, but extremely little which is both affirmative and trustworthy. Madame Campan's short statement remains the basis of other people's longer and more detailed narratives. General La Fayette's full account of the day was burned by his wife during the Terror. Count Fersen's memoirs were also partly destroyed. The Abbé Bossuet had Madame de Tourzel's careful history of that day burned; but in the published memoirs she says that she was in residence that day at Versailles, as *Gouvernante des enfants de France*; she does not mention having gone to Trianon, as implied by Marion's story, but it is still possible. Most French historians now adopt Madame Campan's statement, but (in the words of one of them) 'with some doubts'. It is worth mentioning that many later historians insert the fact (though it is not recorded by Madame Campan) that 'the Queen was accompanied by a single valet'. Is this a tradition?

11. We do not believe in anniversaries in the usual sense. We

have tested both our days (August 10th and January 2nd), going, as far as possible, under the same circumstances, without any result at the Petit Trianon. Yet it is possible that if we entered into an act of memory, it may well have been first made on the terrible 10th of August, 1792, though the memory itself was occupied (in the central place) with the events of October 5th, 1789. The dress of the messenger was more suitable for October than August. At the same time Vaudreuil left France the previous summer and cannot have sat in the Trianon woods after the taking of the Bastille, July 14th, 1789.

There was an incoherence about both the large and small incidents which seems to require combination within a single mind, and the only mind to which they could all have been present would have been that of the Queen. Our theory of 1901, that we had entered within the working of the Queen's memory when she was still alive, is now enlarged. We think that the two first visits to Trianon (August 10th, 1901, and January 2nd, 1902) were part of one and the same experience; that quite mechanically we must have seen it as it appeared to her more than a hundred years ago, and have heard sounds familiar, and even something of words spoken, to her then.

Having been for two most trying years confined to Paris, and (excepting for a visit to St. Cloud) through two hot summers, and being in the midst of the tumultuous horrors of the great tenth of August, she may, as the day wore on, and she grew more used to her miserable position in the Hall of the Assembly—where she sat for eighteen hours—have fancied (in memory) the grounds at Trianon more spacious than they really were; and have seen the trees, as one sees trees in recollection, like a picture without life, depth, or movement. In rêverie her mind may have wandered from the familiar sight of the two Bersys at the gate, to the little vision of two men gathering up garden rubbish into a cart (which we know happened on October 5th, 1789, as well as one day during the last winter she spent at Versailles), and which—

89

without any reason—had remained in her mind. She may have thought of the place as it was during that year of the meeting of the States-General when the grounds were, for the first time, thrown completely open to the public, and intruding strangers could be seen there. Or she may have gone back to the earlier years and the pleasant afternoons when the band played on the *pelouse* in front of the house, and to the excitement of acting in the little theatre with her special friends, perhaps letting herself realise the unkindness of the pressure put upon her by Vaudreuil to have the acting of the *Mariage de Figaro* authorised.

How naturally the thought of him would have formed one picture in her mind with the memory of the last scene, when she was hurriedly summoned from Trianon, never to return! For she may very likely have supposed all that she was suffering to have been more exclusively the result of her own former mistakes than could have been just, and have been going over them in her mind.

On our return to Paris on the day of the original visit to Trianon, when undoubtedly her image was uppermost in our thoughts, and the recollection of her terrible end was hardly to be endured, the recurring consolation to Miss Moberly was, 'She has forgiven it all now, and knows the true meaning of the French Revolution on both its good and bad sides, and also the exact proportion of her own part in it.' But the act of memory which had so strangely and mechanically clung to the place, with which we had, perhaps, been associated in the grounds, was incoherent and pictorial. It was oppressive to us because it represented a more limited view of those times than after a hundred years we have learnt to take of them, and was far more limited than any thought the Queen can have about them now.

12. Our answer to the suggestion that we were in a state of suspended consciousness is that our conversation and sense of the quiet continuity of things remained unbroken, and, in spite of oppression, we believed ourselves to be particularly wide awake and on the alert. When we were first asked whether the man from

Answers to Questions

the side building was real or not, we laughed at the idea of any
unreality; all was so quietly natural that we are still uncertain
whether the tall gardener belonged to another century or not. It
has taken us nine years to work out all the details which bear
witness to the strangeness of what we saw and did, and to justify
us in our present conviction, that from the moment of our leaving the lane until we emerged into the avenue we were on en-
chanted ground.

13. The theory of coincidences would have to be considerably
strained to cover more than twenty points quickly succeeding one
another.

14. In the municipal records kept in the Library at Versailles
there is a list of fêtes in the grounds. Miss Jourdain has examined
it carefully. There had been one for which people had been
dressed in Louis XVI. costume in June, 1901, but there is a note
to say that it had been confined to the Hameau. There was none
in August, 1901. We know that since 1901 there have been fêtes
in the grounds with scenes in character, so that other people may
have come across them; an examination of the records as to dates
would probably reveal such possibilities.

In the same catalogue notices are made of photographs taken
of historical groups at fêtes; there had been some in connection
with the June fête, and 'Otto' was mentioned by name. On enquiry Otto wrote that he had not taken 'l'ensemble de la fête,
c'était des groupes de jeunes filles, et des dames séparément'.
'Dufayel' took pains to look the matter up, and Miss Jourdain and
one of his employées went all through his lists and books of
specimen photographs, and found that he had not taken any
photographs at Trianon between 1900 and 1906. He recom-
mended enquiries at Pierre Petit's, as Petit would have Lafayette's as well as other photographers' pictures. No photographs of
the scenes we wanted were to be heard of there, and Pierre Petit
wrote afterwards that his only photographs at Trianon had been
taken in 1900 for the Exhibition.

91

An Adventure

It has been suggested to us that our story can be explained by people posing for a cinematograph in order to register the scene of the messenger running to the Queen, whilst something further has been said of a girl sweeping up leaves as forming part of the group. Naturally, from the first, we had thought of some such explanation, but had rejected it as insufficient. We did not see the man running; we only heard him; then he suddenly appeared, standing close to us, and addressed us personally, earnestly, and with excitement. As a scene it would have been nothing; we saw no Queen, and no girl sweeping up leaves. He remained by us until we turned away from him. The cinematograph theory does not explain how it was that he came over and stood with his back against rocks of considerable size piled on one another, when rocks have not been there for nearly a hundred years, though we find that they had been placed in that part of the garden in 1788. Nor does it explain how it was that both before and during the man's coming we were both gazing at a kiosk which is not now in existence, though both rocks and kiosk we found out years after to have made part of the original scenery in 1789. Not a word is hinted about the little bridge over the ravine, and the little cascade close by, all being essentials both to our, and, we believe, to the original story. We suspect the explanation to be simply that we had not talked about them at first, not knowing their significance till later, and so they have not got into any widely-spread story. We know from the archives that the streams were not cleared from leaves after October 4th, 1789, and that 'Mariamne' is only mentioned as having been paid for work in the grounds in *1783*, as one of several children so occupied.

If masqueraders were posing as guards at the *porte du jardinier*, the cinematograph idea does not explain the reappearance of the old cottage close by, in its former position as placed in Mique's map of 1783. If the part of the Queen was being acted, what of the orchard of trees we saw her looking into, not now in existence; also, what is the account of the barrier at our right hand screening off the present view and exactly answering to the old enclosure of the Jeu de Bague?

The cinematograph does not explain the man who opened the great door of the chapel, easily hanging it behind him as he came out; for in 1907 the people living in the place believed that it had not been opened since the days of Louis XVI, and the keeper of the key knew that even the door of the landing had not been opened for fifteen years. How was the wall lowered, which now largely hides the great door of the terrace, and makes it necessary to go down one flight of steps and up another, whereas we saw the man coming along a level, in full view, from the moment of his opening the door until he reached us standing on the terrace outside the window of the *antichambre*?[1]

A cinematograph would not explain the reappearance of the old wood in all its denseness; nor the rapid disappearance of the cart and horse in an open field; nor the music, which, six years later, was found to be a piecing together of eighteenth century operas.

No amount of masqueraders explains to us the ease with which we dismissed from sight and hearing the usual August crowds in the middle of a fine afternoon, and the impossibility of harmonising our recollections of the scenery with anything but the old maps and records. Certainly none of the persons we met were being photographed at the moment, or we must have seen it; and had scenery been erected for the purpose, we must have observed such large artificial arrangements; there would probably have been sightseers; and, presumably, the fact of anything so considerable would have been in the catalogue.

Even should it be proved that a cinematograph had been taken that very day, it would not be a possible explanation to us. The groups we saw were small and isolated from one another. There was the deepest silence everywhere, and no sunshine; whilst the

[1] We heard in 1910 that this was the window out of which Marie Antoinette used to pass when she went into the garden.

light was the worst possible for a picture, for the sky was overcast. And though whilst we stood there an indefinable air of strangeness dropped over everything, including the tall forest trees, it was not of a kind that could be accounted for by fictitious scenery. The people moved and spoke as usual, but their words were extraordinarily difficult to catch.

In September, 1910, the question of such representation was settled by an enquiry of the authorities. No leave to take cinematographs had been granted in August, 1901. The fête had been on June 27th, and the photographs of it had been taken sufficiently near the time to be published in the July number of *Versailles Illustré*. Not one of the pictures in this number is in the least like what we saw either in the matter of subjects, costumes, or places. The inaccuracy is so great, that in an article in the same magazine the scene of the messenger coming to the Queen is transferred from the grotto to the Hameau, though the sole authority for the tradition places it at the grotto.

15. During the last five or six years much research into topographical and archæological details has been made by the newly-formed 'Société des amis de Versailles', probably from the same archives examined by Miss Jourdain, so that many points of likeness to what we saw may soon reappear. Old music with old-fashioned instruments is now frequently introduced at summer fêtes at Trianon. Even the water arrangements in our part of the garden seem likely to be altered, and the little cascade may yet be seen again. At the beginning of 1910 Miss Jourdain saw engineers searching for the first and second *sources*, and in the following autumn she found iron grids placed on the ground near the positions we had allotted for them; but nothing had been altered up to September, 1910. We are most curious to know whether the restorations will be exactly according to our recollections of the scenery or not.

16. Stories retailing just so much of our own as we had first talked about are constantly being repeated to us; some with the

little additions we can recognise as our own early surmises; generally with the omission of points we did not know to be interesting until later; and often with all the muddles arising from the attempt to shorten a long story, with a few unauthorised additions and explanations thrown in. These stories are told to us as being the property of persons we have never heard of. We have constantly enquired on what authority they rest, and, if there is any at all, we have not infrequently been able to discover the track they have followed from us back to us again.

17. We do not think that deception explains it. If we were deceived in one, two, or three points, could we have been in all? For out of them we have been able to reconstruct the story of Trianon in many tiny details, the truth of which we have had to discover for ourselves.

18. We are constantly asked why we, of all people, should have had such an adventure? We are equally puzzled; and have come to think that it may not be so unusual as it seems. We can imagine that people, even if they suspected anything unusual (which they might easily not do), may have thought it best not to follow it up. The peculiarity in our case may simply have been that two persons were equally able to consider the circumstances, and did do so: that we found there was available evidence, and that we had the opportunity for obtaining it.

19. Certain unusual conditions were present.

(1) Two people in broad daylight, good health, and normal conditions, were equally able to bear witness to the facts, yet not in the manner of thought transference between each other, for they did not see alike in every point.

(2) Some of the facts were so small that no historical knowledge, however dim, could have suggested them.

(3) They concerned such well known historical personages that much documentry proof as to the reality of the incidents is accessible; yet, in some particulars, they are of such a nature as to be incapable of reproduction by any tricks of scenic effects; and

some of the evidence found in the archives had, to all appearance, not been disturbed since its collection by the National Assembly until Miss Jourdain in 1904 undid the old fastenings that had stuck together through age and disuse: for instance—much of the evidence about the gardeners taken from the wages-book.

C.A.E.M.

E.F.J.

September, 1910

CHAPTER IV

A Rêverie

A POSSIBLE HISTORICAL CLUE

To find the causes of the universal movement, which for convenience we call the French Revolution, one should be a trained historian, philosopher, and theologian, and be able to pass in review and justly estimate the aspirations for political consolidation, greater individual responsibility, and the revolt against Papal tyranny over consciences, as they had been working in all European countries for many centuries. To find the causes for the particular form which this universal development took in France, it would be necessary to weigh the moral, social, and political (including the fiscal) tendencies of earlier generations. This would be manifestly impossible in a paper dealing with the revolution in France as it may have appeared to a single mind, on one special day, at a time of great mental excitement. There can be no doubt that Marie Antoinette was the innocent victim of a world-wide upheaval in the moments when men were first consciously developing it, and we can well believe that to herself the reasons for such reversals of older thoughts seemed inscrutable; whilst she would have vainly sought, in reflecting over her own mistakes, for grounds sufficient to justify the enormous misfortunes which overwhelmed her personally.

The tenth of August, 1792, was a marked day in the history of the French Revolution. The tide of French democratic reaction against the ever-increasing selfishness of privilege, and the inability of the rulers to sympathise with the growing desire for greater freedom and less personal government, had been gathering force with constantly increasing momentum; and on this day Louis XVI virtually relinquished all independence as Head of the State by surrendering himself, for the sake of the safety of his family and to save France from the crime of massacring its King, into the doubtful care of the Legislative Assembly.

That Assembly grew out of the States-General which had been convened by the King, May 5th, 1789, at one of the critical moments when the dissatisfaction of the nation with its financial conditions produced keen anxiety to the Court; and it had (on another epoch-making day of that unrestful period) refused, on June 23rd, 1789, to be dissolved by mandate of the King. From that moment the National Assembly had become the centre of the reforming party in France. Louis XVI., as King, did not seem to stand in the way of the wishes of the nation as expressed by the Assembly. He appeared to be willing to forgo more of his prerogatives than was compatible with the existence of monarchy as understood in France; but, it was believed, the Queen was of a different opinion and desirous of upholding the ancient monarchical idea as a practical force, which at that time, in spite of the King's amiability and absence of policy, could not be otherwise than hostile to the still vague, but unbounded, aspirations of the democratic party. 'Madame Veto' had that influence over the King due to a strong personality and her position as a much loved wife; upon her, therefore, fell the wrath of the nation. It was instinctively recognised that as a wife and mother she had every reason to desire the continuance of things as they were, and the people quickly interpreted every act of vacillation on the King's part to the Queen's active enmity to the rising forces of democracy.

It was on August 10th, 1792, that the Legislative Assembly was made to realise another function belonging to it beyond that of fighting the prerogatives of the King and of the aristocracy. In such a restless age, and in such a country as France, it was

A Rêverie

impossible to suppose that the outspoken longings of philosophers, poets, and statesmen for freedom, should not stir up the hope of freedom from all authority and restraint whatever in the lowest stratum of society. The lengths to which the mob in Paris could go had, during the last three years, shown itself on isolated occasions, but with increasing frequency and savagery. Both mob and Assembly were animated by the same desire, viz. to make monarchy in France absolutely helpless to withstand their will. The Assembly was trying to bring it about with some appearance of constitutional decency, without apparently perceiving that unless the King was allowed to banish himself, a discrowned monarch without any *raison d'être* whatever in the country inevitably meant his ultimate, and perhaps speedy, disappearance by death. The mob saw its policy more clearly, and was ready to get rid of him and the Queen by instant murder.

Thus, on the morning of August 10th, the Legislative Assembly had the double part to play of continuing its assault on privilege whilst protecting the royal family from destruction.

When, at some moment between 7 and 9 a.m., Louis XVI and Marie Antoinette entered the Manège in which the Council met, there was, at first, some attempt at restrained courtesy showing itself in the grave assurance of protection in reply to the King's request, and also in half an hour's doubt as to where he should sit down. But the Assembly was entirely aware of its victory in this act of unconditional surrender on the part of the King, and would allow no royal guards of any description to enter. There was a short alarm lest it should have to defend itself against the cannon of the insurgents, the sound of firing approaching nearer to the building than the nerves of some of the deputies could sustain with calmness.[1] But the mob had not yet realised that it had the upper hand, and was content to believe that the protected King was the imprisoned King, and only continued to howl ferocious threats outside the *grilles*.

[1] Lenotre, *Marie Antoinette*, p. 3.

An Adventure

If the Assembly did not immediately see its way to the definite imprisonment of the Sovereign, neither did it choose that the royal party should sit on its own benches, so it ordained that they should be placed in the *logographie*—the reporter's room—a sort of den not far from the President's chair, open to the Manège and within sight and hearing of all that passed, but without dignity or decent comfort.[1] Here, without apparently any opportunity for resting or meals, the King, Queen, Princess Elizabeth, Madame Royale, and the Dauphin remained, until (at least) 10 p.m.[2] A few faithful attendants, such as the Princesse de Lamballe, Madame de Tourzel, the Prince de Poix, and the Duc de la Rochefoucauld, were with them, and at first other royalists were allowed to bring them news and to pass in and out, but this was stopped in the course of the day.

From Dufour's account it would seem that no one was busying themselves to supply their wants until he undertook to do so the next day.[3] A draught of water brought to them in their cells at night to quench their raging thirst is all that he speaks of. If the story of the King eagerly devouring food in public is true (and it is impossible to believe that the children had nothing), yet it is doubtful whether the Queen, who had had no rest the night before, had any food during the day.

What a tumult of disgust, fears, indignation, and overwhelming regrets must have occupied the Queen's mind! It was difficult enough to maintain an outwardly calm, queenly demeanour; her thoughts must have been confused, half formed, reflecting the agitation of despair and anxiety. She knew only too well that she was looked upon as the political enemy of the crowd for reasons that were not altogether untrue. She had had a policy inconsistent with republicanism and, though worsted in it, the events of the last three years probably justified it in her own mind.

[1] *Mémoires de Madame de Tourzel*, p. 216.
[2] Rocheterie says 18 hours; Dufour, 13 hours.
[3] Lenotre, *Marie Antoinette*, p. 13.

A Rêverie

She inherited a belief in a strong rule, beneficent as her own kindly nature required, but one that could fight its battles and make full use of such opportunities as hereditary kingship possessed. Again and again she had felt that the King's action was worse than nothing. Marie Antoinette would have sternly punished the crime of killing the King's officials;[1] she would have upheld the sovereign office as long as there were those who prized it. The country could never have reached the present point of rebellion, if the taking of the Bastille, for instance, had not been condoned and the murders and outrages connected with it had not been allowed to pass without adequate punishment. Why were the troops dismissed so soon after, and the nobles allowed to emigrate? It may have been right for the monarch to urge upon some of them the danger in which they stood by remaining, but where was their courage and loyalty in leaving the country?[2]

The sensation of loneliness was terrible. Where were the illustrious families and statesmen who had not left France, who, had the Queen only known it, were to go during the next year in one long procession to the scaffold? They were, she knew, paralysed by the King's inaction and weakness. Surely they would have rallied had he called upon them with decision to defend their rights and had placed himself at their head, even though many of those princely families who had surrounded her during the first years of her reign had been alienated and in opposition to herself before the disaffection became general. Where were the faithful Swiss guards who only that morning had escorted them in safety to the Manège, and would have fought bravely and perhaps been the rallying point for all who were not declared democrats? Alas,

[1] De Launay; governor of the Bastille,
Flescelles; prévôt des marchands, } July 14, 1789.
Foulon; ministre,
Berthier; intendant de l'Ile de France, } July 4, 1789.

[2] Le Comte d'Artois, les Condés, les Polignacs, le Baron de Breteuil, le maréchal de Broglie, le prince de Lambesc, le comte de Vaudreuil, les ministres Barenton, Villedeuil, Vauguyon, l'abbé de Vermond.

101

alas, the sounds of screams and fiendish massacre were in her ears at the moment; cannon, musketry and cold-blooded carnage were then and there destroying the last stronghold! The tiny *loge*, only 10 feet square, so painfully hot and full of comers and goers, seemed to the despairing Queen empty of all who should have been there to represent the monarchical principle. The presence of the Prince de Poix and the Duc de la Rochefoucauld and a few others, who were endangering their lives by being with them, only emphasised the forlornness of the royal condition.

Looking from her dismal corner in the *loge* at the King, who sat with impassive mien facing the assembly, what waves of painful emotion must have swept across her brain! The King could not see things from her point of view, but he had loved and spoilt her. He had been faithful to her, as no French monarch for many generations had been loyal to his wife. He was devoted to her and to their children; had paid her debts again and again;[1] had enobled and enriched her friends; his patience and magnanimity were saintly; but how often had she raged against his theory that the King's duty was to set an example of lofty forbearance and forgiveness of every injury even when done to him as representing the law, justice, and power of the whole French peoples. She had instinctively felt that had she been in the King's place she would have found her way through the past crises without either descending from her throne or doing wrong to the most Christian charity. She knew that she was kind-hearted, and had always loved to be the benefactress of others: yes, she too could forgive royally when forgiveness was due from her in her own person, but not when it required injustice to others.

---

[1] In 1783 the Queen's wardrobe cost 199,000 livres; in 1784 it cost 217,000 livres; in 1785 it cost 252,000. One dress only worn once cost 6000 livres, not counting the material. *La Reine Marie Antoinette*, De Nolhac, pp. 36, 63.

In 1777 the Queen's personal debts amounted to 487,000 livres, which the King paid out of his own purse. All this was changed after the birth of her first child, and the Queen, from that time, cut down every possible expense.

A Rêverie

But Marie Antoinette was too clear-sighted to impute all the blame of this downfall to the King's mistakes. No doubt his feeble idea had been to behave as though the democrats only were the nation, forgetting the contrary view of those who had either banished themselves or who were perforce silent unless he could lead the way. To obey every behest of the Legislative Assembly and of the mob showed a lamentable lack of wisdom, but even such a poor policy had brought him an undoubted though fleeting popularity. He had appeared to take the side of the opponents of monarchy; he had divested himself of prerogatives; had sworn to a Constitution beyond his power to carry out, and had submitted to the indignity of placing the red bonnet on his head; but had she not helped to make all this short-sighted weakness even more unavailing than it need have been? What was the use of humbling the aristocracy along with himself, and of acting against his own convictions, if at the same time he consented to plans for escaping, and was known to be so far untrustworthy to his own professions that at every crisis he listened to her incessant urgings to the more spirited policy, by which he could instantly rally the royal forces?

Bitterly she knew that she had never prevailed to overcome his fatal belief that the King was never to shed the blood of a Frenchman, even if he were a disturber of the public peace; but she had ever to bear the blame of every mistake. She thought of that terrible message sent only two hours ago at the bidding of the Assembly that their guards were not to defend themselves, but to disarm.[1] Only this morning there were 600 Swiss and 200 gentlemen, and even companies of the national guard whom they could trust, but whispered reports had reached even the *loge* that their noble supporters had died unsoldierly and cold-blooded deaths. There was no longer any nucleus in the country of loyalty to the consecrated ruler.

There was nothing now to prevent the passing of the formal

[1] *Mémoires de Madame de Tourzel*, p. 220.

decree by which she heard the King finally deprived of the crown
and of every vestige of authority. Though Louis XVI. appeared
unheeding and expressionless, could *she* bear this indignity, this
wrong to her son? Could they not escape from this wicked dur-
ance? But she had consented to this surrender to their enemies in
the hope of saving her son's life. It had been the only chance. As
long as they were in some shelter from the howling savages outside who were screaming for their blood, the life of her son was
secure. She had long accustomed herself to the thought of being
assassinated, but there was no fear of a judicial murder; no
government of France would sink to such a point of wickedness
and unwisdom in the face of a united Europe.[1] They would be
condemned to more years of miserable bondage, but they would
be together; friends would rally; circumstances would clear
themselves. The Queen had it in her still to do and dare everything if there were any hope of surmounting the present crisis.

If she might only act! But no, the Queen's heart sank again as
the numbing sense of helplessness came over her, remembering
that she would not be allowed to act. It was always the King who
had the last word. She might plan, but he, with all his love and
confidence in her, invariably thwarted every attempt requiring
some spirit of defiance. He had ruined the Varennes scheme by
letting himself be recognised at critical moments. Why did he
review the guards that morning, and make it unavailing by
omitting to speak words of courage and confidence? Why did he
seek the protection of his enemies rather than fire on the mob,
which an hour later fled away at the volleys fired by the Swiss?[2]
No, there was no hope of contending against the difficulties im-
posed on their party by the inertia of the King. And now things
had gone so far, perhaps he had no choice but to advise obedience
when the Assembly decreed that the few friends outside their

[1] Even in the Conciergerie the Queen seems to have disbelieved in
the likelihood of a formal condemnation to death.—Lenotre, *Marie
Antoinette*, pp. 247,270.
[2] La Rocheterie, p. 435.

A Rêverie

household who had pressed into the *loge* should no longer hold communication with them, but should retire. More than once during those sad hours they had to see faithful servants bleeding and with torn clothes judged at the bar of the Assembly for having defended them.[1] The handkerchief that was handed to the Queen in the place of her own, which was soaked with tears, in order that she might wipe the drops of sweat off the brow of the young Dauphin, was tinged with blood.[2]

Exhausted by horror and disappointment, what strength remained to the Queen must have spent itself in thoughts for her little son, who with touching obedience was trying to be 'bien sage avec ces vilains hommes'.[3] If she was personally helpless to save his crown, surely the Kings of Europe would see to it. Again hope revived at the thought of a successful war already beginning. The false moves of the last years perhaps only meant at the worst that, though she and the King had to die at the hands of an enraged but defeated France, the boy would escape. With victorious armies surrounding Paris, there would be those within who would then be roused to get the lad into the protection of friends. Surely God would help him then!

But what if everything should fail? Fatality had overtaken every reasonable hope since this terrible revolution had begun. There were forces of mysterious and terrific magnitude, which seemed to her to be bearing away everything that had been stable hitherto. Her ignorance of what constituted these forces increased their terror for her. During the two hours when the deputies separately repeated the words of the oath to maintain liberty, equality, or die, the Queen in utter weariness tried to penetrate the mystery of that fatality which seemed to overtake royalty in France, and herself in particular. Perhaps for a

---

[1] Vicomte de Maillé, sent to L'Abbaye prison, murdered in the September massacres. M. de la Porte, *intendant de la liste civile*, also imprisoned and murdered in September. *Mémoires de Madame de Tourzel*, p. 226.
[2] La Rocheterie, p. 438.   [3] La Rocheterie, p. 438.

105

moment she realised that had she seriously studied history some light might have come as to the meaning of this crushing movement. The volumes of Hume's *History of England*, which in early days had been carelessly listened to, conveyed little to her inattentive mind.[1] She did not know even the history of France intelligently enough to be able to guess whether the enveloping force owed its strength to anything which could have been foreseen. Was there anyone who could have foreseen this trend of events, when it was only last year that the Constitution had been applauded to the skies as the consummation of political wisdom?[2]

Was the penury of the country and the starving condition of the poor at the bottom of this earthquake? But why visit them upon the Court? People must know that she and the King were most kindly and anxious and troubled for all. They had reduced every possible expense in their household. Had she not nine years ago refused the diamond necklace on account of its expense? She had not gambled in old days more than others; neither had she enriched her friends more than sovereigns were in the habit of doing. The Pompadours and Dubarrys had rolled in wealth. What was the cost of Trianon compared to the millions of money spent in building the Palace of Versailles?[3] It was unjust to make her and her children bear the punishment of the sins of former generations.

Were such writers as Voltaire and Rousseau responsible in any degree for the gathering forces that were crashing all law and order as they had been hitherto understood? The Queen knew something of their views, but their invectives against kings as

---

[1] Nolhac, *La Reine Marie Antoinette*, p. 184.

[2] *Almanach Historique de la Révolution Française pour l'année* 1792, par M. J. P. Rabaut (contemporain).

[3] The exterior masonry of the Palace cost 1,350,000 livres, apart from all the magnificent interiors, the grounds, and the outside buildings. La Grande Écurie cost 844,784 livres. (Peraté, *Versailles*, p. 14.) Expenses at Trianon under Louis XV., 340,000 livres; under Louis XVI., 1,649,529 livres. (Desjardins, pp. 2, 407.)

tyrants seemed unjust and exaggerated, and had repelled her. To her mind, her mother, husband, and brothers were not selfish oppressors; they meant to be useful to their subjects, and would have been unwise to have rejected the wisdom of former times embodied in traditions and old customs. Moreover, any truths uttered by Voltaire were vitiated to the Queen by his declared hostility to religion as she knew it. Such overwhelming forces as were destroying France could not be the outcome of such feeble views; there must be stronger reasons than such writings could account for.

But here there was some tangle of ideas which could not be unravelled. The Queen's mind was not one to dwell on abstractions; it was wholly untrained and incapable of thinking out points of philosophical or religious argument. She could not disentangle the various points of view which distracted her mind.

As the long hours went on, her sorrows which admitted of no comfort: the strange impassiveness of the king: the sight of her weeping companions: the efforts of the children not to give trouble: and the physical suffering entailed on all alike, boxed up in this stifling hole on a hot August afternoon, filled her with maddening oppression, whilst the cold and insolent words of the hostile Assembly, the unspeakable insults incessantly hurled at her by the cruel voices outside, the noise, the heat, the smells, the want of room, added to the effects of sleepless nights and absence of nourishment, must have filled her with an uncontrollable longing to get away. As the afternoon wore on with no hope of relief, black, helpless despair closed in on the mind of the tired Queen. She must have felt that, if she was not to go mad, it was necessary to extricate herself from her present surroundings by at least a semi-unconsciousness of them. Her brain was on fire. Could she not force her imagination to take some rest? Even in happy times some natural impatience in the Queen's nature made it imperative to her to run away and be alone sometimes.

An Adventure

It was at the Petit Trianon that she had found relief from tiresome restrictions, importunities of etiquette, and obsequious crowds. There at least she could have her own way and her love of simple pleasures and country freedom had been satisfied. If only she could fly to that beloved spot away from this horrible smell of blood, what happiness it would be to her jaded spirits! Only to think of it afforded her a dim pleasure overcoming the inevitable bitterness of the recollection.

Yes; it was the Petit Trianon which of all places in France she loved best. The bare memory of its trees and grass and cool shadows brought a little refreshment. It was there that she had always found a reprieve from the stately formalities of Versailles and that she had been able to unqueen herself and be on an equality with her friends. But was there no pang as she realised with fresh point that the King had just been deposed, and that she, by the voice of the only authority at present recognised in the country, was no longer Queen of France? That favourite pastime of pretending to be no queen in the privacy of Trianon had been a dangerous game! Marie Antoinette had not attempted to be on an equality with the old *haute noblesse* whose absence at this moment was so deplorable. Such familiarity would have lowered them in their own eyes; for their rank and consideration rested on their service to the sovereigns, and only by etiquettes rigorously kept could the princes and old nobility find their own *raison d'être*. With keen pain the truth flashed upon her that a thoughtless Queen had done her best to undermine Cardinal Richelieu's policy in bringing the great feudal princes to squabble in small rivalries about positions at Court rather than leave them to combine into factions and fight each other in wars dangerous to the State. Etiquettes had been laughed at, and the nobles superseded in her favour by persons without claim to the titles and fortunes lavished upon them. But was it possible that such small considerations had really alienated the most powerful class in France? The Queen had only to recollect the restrained indig-

A Rêverie

nation of the Comtesse de Noailles: those dismal years when no one attended her balls at Versailles[1]; the immense offence given to the distinguished families of Soubise, Condé, Rohan, Guemenée, and all who were connected with them, by her furious and undignified anger with Cardinal Rohan:[2] besides the murmurs of all who considered themselves wronged by their exclusion from her friendship at Trianon to realise bitterly what had alienated the aristocracy from her, beyond, apparently, hope of recall.

Too worn and sad to pursue such painful thoughts, it was a relief to let the vision of her favourite home float before her mind's eye and to remember the loyalty of her Trianon servants, such as Antoine Richard, *jardinier en chef*, who had succeeded to the post so long held by his father Claude Richard.[3] How loyally they had carried out her wishes, and, under the direction of her architect Mique,[4] had altered their much loved nursery gardens into a fashionable 'jardin anglais'! It had been delightful planning that garden and altering the arrangements and decorations of the house and grounds with her own rare good taste, until scarcely any part was left bringing to mind the sojourn there of Madame de Pompadour, but the house itself,[5] and the little ménagerie with its vacherie, bergerie, and poulaillers,[6] or of Madame du Barry, but the formal French garden,[7] and the chapel,[8] with the kitchens beyond.

In the stuffy dirty *loge* the royal family had resigned itself to a melancholy silence, the Dauphin was sleeping across her knee,

---

[1] 1777–1779.   [2] 1786.
[3] Claude Richard was appointed *jardinier en chef* at Trianon in 1750. He was the intimate friend of Linnæus, who called him 'the cleverest gardener in Europe'. He was the son of François Richard who followed James II from Windsor to St. Germains. The son, Antoine Richard, became *jardinier-botaniste-adjoint* at Trianon, 1765, *jardinier en chef*, 1784–1805, and died 1807.
[4] Guillotined 1794.
[5] Built 1762.   [6] *Le Petit Trianon*, Desjardins, p. 27.
[7] 1759–1761.   [8] Built 1773 for Madame du Barry.

and the Queen surrendered herself to a trance-like condition in which she saw again with extreme vividness and longing the place of former enjoyment. She was again free, opening all the gates with her own *passe-partout*,[1] and wandering into all the corners of the grounds. The beautiful trees planted by the two Richards in rich variety were, she recollected, in full summer foliage, and she would fain have felt some breath of the cool evening air, which she knew well must be blowing at that moment, though not for her. Or she was again in the mazy wood beyond the Vergelay bridge following in thought the sound of the light operatic music, so often played on bright afternoons, which drifted past her as she made her way along the wood paths. Well-known bars of Monsigny's music mingled with reminiscences of Sacchini's and Grétry's operas. Was it not on an August day, twelve years ago, that she first acted herself in the charming little newly-built theatre?[2] It was in a play of Sedaine (*Le Roi et le Fermier*) for which Monsigny had written music, especially for the Trianon; and with pain it was remembered that the plot of the play was the favourite one at Trianon, viz. the superiority of the farmer's condition over that of the King. Vaudreuil had acted the part of the farmer lover to her Jenny. The Queen's thoughts flew to another, and the last, acting,[3] so immediately followed by the frightful episode of the diamond necklace when outrage first touched her and personal popularity was finally lost.[4] Under pressure from the Comte de Vaudreuil she had prevailed with the King, against his better judgment, to allow the *Mariage de Figaro* to be acted in Paris.[5] In the following year, the older version of the same play had been performed

---

[1] 'Avoir netoyer le passe-partout que la Reine avait perdue avoir gravée de nom de la Reine dessus qui ouvrait les portes du Chateau et jardin de Trianon.' Locksmith's account, 1785 (*Archives Nat.* O¹, 1882).

[2] August 1st, 1780.   [3] August 19th, 1785.

[4] Cardinal Rohan had been arrested four days before, on August 15th, 1785.

[5] Beaumarchais' play of *Le Mariage de Figaro* had been rewritten with political intention from the old play of *Le Barbier de Séville* in 1783.

A Rêverie

at Trianon;[1] she had acted Rosina, the Comte d'Artois had taken the part of Figaro, and Vaudreuil that of Almaviva. Four years later the King's prophecy had come true, and the destruction of the Bastille had been the signal for Vaudreuil's hurried flight from the country.[2]

Well she remembered that false friend,[3] whom she had willingly received into her most intimate circle, though latterly he had often wearied her with his violent temper and importunities for more lucrative posts.[4]

There was one day in that last summer at Trianon, shortly before Vaudreuil's final departure in July, which stood out, every detail being imprinted on her memory. She had wandered up the lane past the *logement du corps de garde*, and had noticed on the ground near the lodge gates the old plough—a reminiscence of Louis XVI's boyhood.[5] Coming towards the *porte du jardinier*, she had seen Rodolphe and Fidel Bersy[6] in the long green coats of the *petite livrée* of the *gardes*.[7] They were directing some strangers. These guards were special friends of hers. Had she not paid all expenses out of her own purse when Rodolphe's children had been ill with smallpox?[8] Whilst passing them she had noticed Marie Anne Lemaignan[9] standing near her

[1] Twice played at Trianon, September 13th, 1784, and August 19th, 1785.
[2] July 14th, 1789.
[3] Nolhac, *La Reine Marie Antoinette*, pp. 161–212, 223, 224.
[4] Desjardins, pp. 180, 178, 342.   [5] Rocheterie, pp. 289, 290, vol. i.
[6] The brothers Bersy with Bréval were generally selected for guarding the *porte du jardinier* whenever the Queen was at Trianon, *Arch. Nat.* O¹, 1880. They had the title of *garçons jardiniers de la Chambre*, O¹, 1878.
[7] Probably green, as it was worn by the Suisses, piqueurs, gardes des portes, garçons jardiniers, and such royal servants as filled the minor parts at the royal theatre at Versailles, *Arch. Nat.* O¹, 1883. The traditional dress is still to be seen at the Comédie Française, which is the descendant of the old Royal Theatre. The Comte d'Artois was captain of the guards (including the gardes des portes) in 1789, and his livery was green.
[8] In 1785, *Arch. Nat.* O¹, 1883.
[9] The names 'Lemonguin' and 'Magny' are to be found in the old lists of under-gardeners at Trianon, *Arch. Nat.* O¹, 1876, 1877. Mariamne

111

An Adventure

mother[1] on the steps of their cottage outside the enclosure.[2] The Queen calculated that the girl, who had then been fourteen years old,[3] must now be a young woman of seventeen, and with her promise of beauty[4] would soon marry: probably, she thought, to young Charpentier,[5] who was already, she knew, attached to the girl. The Queen's intimacy with her servants at Trianon had been a never-failing happiness, and she thought with infinite tenderness of the troubles their loyal sympathy for her must be causing them now.

Passing through the gardeners' enclosure and the *porte d'entrée* she had come into the English garden. Advancing a few steps, she had suddenly caught sight of Vaudreuil sitting by the small circular 'ruine',[6] dressed, she remembered, in the slouch hat and

is mentioned among the children paid for picking up dead leaves in the grounds, 1783, *Arch. Nat.* O¹, 1877.

[1] Marion's mother died shortly before 1793. Lavergne, *Légendes de Trianon.*

[2] In Mique's map of 1783 there is a building outside the wall between the *ruelle* and the *porte de jardiner.*

[3] If Marianne was 21 at her son's birth in 1796 she would have been 8 in 1783, and 14 in 1789.

[4] In 1793 'Marion' (daughter of an under-gardener) was chosen by the Versailles Republican Club to personate the local Goddess of Reason. Horrified at the prospect, the night before the installation on the altar of the Versailles Notre Dame, she so completely disfigured her face with scratches from a thorn branch that she never completely lost the marks. *Ibid.*, pp. 91–97.

[5] In 1786 'Charpantier' is mentioned as an *ouvrier terrassier*, having to clear up sticks and leaves, plant flowers, and rake (*Arch. Nat.* O¹, 1878).
Charpentier seems to have been the 'Jean de l'eau,' so called from his daily duty of fetching water from Ville d'Avray for the Queen's table. He even tried to get it to her when she was in the Conciergerie, August, 1792. He was afterwards wounded at Marengo and became a captain, and in 1805 was appointed by Napoleon *jardinier en chef* at the Petit Trianon, and married Marion (Lavergne p. 97).
The marriage certificate of Alexandre Charpentier, in 1823 (at that time *chef d'atelier aux Pépinières Royales* de Trianon, and, later, for many years *jardinier en chef* at Trianon), shows that he was the son of Louis Toussaint Charpentier, *pensionnaire*, and Marie Anne Lemaignan (Mairie de Versailles).

[6] 'Dec. 5, 1780. Commencé par ordre de M. Mique le model de la partie de la grotte . . . du coté des montagnes . . . là dessus une petite ruine d'architecture, l'avoir penté, planté, et gazonné.'
'Detail estimatif d'une ruine formant la naissance d'une rivière,

112

large cloak which had become fashionable since he had acted as such in Almaviva.[1] He turned and looked at her, but did not rise or make the smallest gesture of recognition. It was by her own orders that at Trianon her ladies and gentlemen did not rise or put away their occupations when the Queen entered a room; but she had lately become sensitive, and on this occasion she had felt his rudeness.[2] After all, she was the Queen; he was there as her honoured guest, where the highest in the land desired to be, and ordinary good manners required him to do more than sit still and look at her without seeming to notice her. The Queen remembered her sensation of displeasure. And now her extraordinarily excited memory which was enabling her to see Trianon again down to the smallest details of the scenery, also revealed to her her short-sighted folly in undermining the first principles of that mutual courtesy which constitutes best Court life, at a time when France was on the verge of an immense political whirlpool.

Yes; it was on that very same spot that the messenger came to her, a few months later, to announce the crowd of disaffected

savoir—Fouille de terre—maçonnerie . . . le massif et le rigolle des fondations . . . pierre dure . . . colonnes avec les murs au derrière . . . 7 colonnes . . . 7 chapiteaux . . . partie de la voute . . . le parement des murs . . . le fossite pour l'architecture . . . Récapitulation . . . 7 chapiteaux Ioniques, antique . . . 5 membres . . . 5 rosaces . . . 9358 livres" (*Arch. Nat.* O[1], 1878.)

The Temple de l'Amour is more than once called a 'ruine', which did not seem to mean more than the reproduction of an older building. One 'ruine' mentioned had six Corinthian pillars, and was near the 'onze arpents'.

[1] 'Le chapeau rond à larges bords, que l'on appelait à la jockey, remplaçait déjà le chapeau à trois cornes nommé à l'Androsmane.' On avait quitté le rabat, la bourse, les manchettes et l'épée.' Reiset, *Modes et Usages*, vol. i, p. 469.

[2] 'J'ai beaucoup vu le comte de Vaudreuil à Londres, sans avoir jamais découvert la distinction dont ses contemporains lui ont fait honneur. Il avait été le coryphée de cette école d'exagération qui régnait avant la Révolution, se passionnant pour toutes les petites choses, et restant froide devant les grandes . . . Il . . . gardait ses grands airs pour le salon de Madame de Polignac; et son ingratitude pour la Reine, dont je l'ai entendu parler avec la dernière inconvenance' (*Mémoires de la Comtesse de Boigne*, p. 144).

An Adventure

women from Paris *en route* for Versailles. She could never forget that October morning, for from that time her life had entirely altered in character and the Queen had endured a weary round of perpetual and open insult. Throughout the preceding summer the grounds at the Petit Trianon, which had formerly been so jealously guarded even from the Court, had been thrown open to the public,[1] and in order to take the chance of walking there in any privacy the Queen had lately been in the habit of driving over during the morning. That fifth of October had been fairly fine during the early hours, and she remembered having seen the gardeners at work in the different parts of the gardens;[2] and on her way from the Temple de l'Amour to the Hameau, she had passed the *prairie*, and had seen two labourers in their picturesque brown tunics and coloured *chaperons rouges*[3] filling a hired cart with sticks.[4]

Crossing the Vergelay bridge she had approached the cavernous mouth of her favourite grotto,[5] over which ivy fell in graceful wreaths.[6] For the first time in her experience she had noticed that the little stream issuing from the grotto had not been cleared,

[1] Desjardins, p. 345.

[2] The wages book shows that all the gardeners were at work out of doors on Oct. 5th, 1789, whereas on wet days they worked under cover, sometimes clearing out the passages of the house (*Arch. Nat.* O[1], 1879).

[3] This was the dress of the bourgeoisie in the fourteenth century. See illustration of fourteenth century play *Pathelin*. Artisans wore it in the seventeenth century. See *Les Foires des Rues de Paris*. Musée Carnavalet. It was probably worn by field labourers up to the Revolution.

[4] There is no mention of a cart and horse as part of the regular expenses at the Ferme, but from time to time 'une voiture à un cheval, et un conducteur' were hired for picking up sticks in the Park. Jan., 1789, there is an entry for paying 'plus un homme' for that purpose; and on Oct. 4th, 1789, we read of the hiring of 'trois journées de voiture et deux chevaux' (almost necessarily requiring two men) (O[1], 1843).

[5] See old picture by L'Espinasse, 1783. In Mique's map (1783) two grottos are indicated, one close to the rocher bridge, on the left of it coming from the Hameau, and one near the Escargot hill, still to be seen today.

[6] May 28th, 1781 ... Ont attachés le lierre de la grotte (O[1], 1875).

A Rêverie

but was choked with dead autumn leaves.[1] This unusual and forlorn sight had remained in her mind. Here she had sat for a time looking at the place now deserted by all who had formerly been with her there, and, as was inevitable at that time of political anxiety, became engrossed in mournful anticipations of further troubles.[2] They had pressed more than she could bear, and feeling a sudden desire to speak to someone she had entered the moss-lined grotto.[3] Passing the point on her left hand where the little cascade entered from above,[4] she climbed the rock stair-

[1] The streams were cleared of dead leaves on October 1st, 2nd, 3rd, but not on the 4th or 5th or after that date (O[1], 1877).

[2] Madame Campan, *Memoirs of Marie Antoinette*, p. 201. Julie Lavergne, *Légendes de Trianon*, p. 75.

[3] In the time of Marie Antoinette there were at least three grottos at Trianon, of which only one remains intact, and that possibly the last created; it may have been formed along with the Escargot hill, raised in 1781 (*Arch. Nat.* O[1], 1877).

The oldest grotto is mentioned in 1777 as ending at the *porte d'entrée* (O[1], 1875). Issuing from the side of this first grotto was a 'naissance de rivière', which fed (perhaps by pipes) the small circular lake, whose waters passed under the Rocher bridge, through the great lake to the stream which meandered through the grounds. A small 'ruine' having seven columns, a dome roof, and walls, stood above the spring 'formant la naissance de la rivière' (O[1], 1878, Desjardins, p. 90).

Such waters as drained naturally through the first grotto seem to have collected in a little pool at the lower end. In June, 1780, a new 'petite rivière', intended to carry these stagnant waters away direct to the great lake, was made; a grotto of 'oval form' was dug round it, and a montagne raised to cover it in (O[1], 1875). This second grotto was probably the one described by d'Hezecques: it must have turned at an angle from the first grotto and ended near the Rocher bridge, the tiny ruisseau passing through and beyond it into the great lake (O[1], 1875).

[4] A small ravine between the first and second grottos may have been spanned by the 'pont rustique' of d'Hezecques, passing over the miniature waterfall issuing from 'la 2ième source du Ravin' (nearer the Theatre than the first spring) (O[1], 1882). This would have given the name 'ravin du petit pont' (O[1], 1875). The waterfall probably fell into the little pool, whose waters were carried by a 'ruisseau' through the second (the Queen's) grotto to the great lake. A rough sketch in the *Arch. Nat.* shows a small bridge in this position.

The cavern-like mouth at the lower end of the Queen's grotto, close to the Rocher bridge, is shown in L'Espinasse's picture of 1783. It is to be observed that in this picture no large rock (such as there is now) was over the long bridge which stood upon low rocks between the two lakes. The picture suggests that the rock opening of the grotto has been lifted away from its original place to its present position over the long Rocher bridge.

An Adventure

case[1] leading to the upper opening[2] near the *porte d'entrée*. Coming out upon the elevated rocks, she called to Marie Anne Lamaignan, whose father's cottage was not far off. Fancying that she heard the girl running to her, the Queen had turned and was surprised to see, instead of the girl, a *garçon de la Chambre*, who, in a state of great agitation, handed her a letter from M. de Saint Priest, a minister at the Palace.[3] Her memory recalled the look of that man, also in the fashionable Spanish hat and cloak, flying over one of the upright rocks placed near the path by her orders.[4] He had been so anxious that she should wait at the house whilst he fetched the carriage that she relinquished her first thought of hurrying back by the woods, and she turned instead to go to the little bridge which crossed the tiny waterfall. How fond she was of that little rustic bridge, which she had had placed high up on rocks, hiding the Theatre and surrounded by thujas and pine trees![5] It had been one of the most charming of her inventions, and in fancy the Queen again saw every step of the way, and the

[1] d'Hezecques describes the grotto as dark on first entering, lined with moss, and as having a staircase within it leading to the summit of the rocks. This staircase may be identical with the rock staircase now attached by modern masonry to the back of the great rock over the bridge, without any apparent reason.

[2] A view of the prairie (also a condition of the Queen's grotto described by d'Hezecques) is obtainable from the high ground in this part of the English garden.

[3] Julie Lavergne, *Légendes de Trianon*, p. 76.

[4] (Rocks placed) 'Pièce donnant au bord du lac de l'ancien jardin cote des rochers ... au long du chemin de l'emplacement de la Ruine sur la conduitte en bois à la 2ième Source du Ravin' (O¹, 1882).

In 1788 'Pièce au dessus du Rocher du Ravin et ... passage des voiture sur le pont de bois ... Pièce à droite en face du Rocher du Ravin.'

[5] 'En face du chateau ... une pelouse ... se terminait par une roche ombragée de pins, de thujas, de mélèzes, et surmontait d'un pont rustique, comme on en rencontre dans les montagnes de la Suisse et les précipices du Valais ... (*Souvenirs d'un Page*, p. 242).

(Rocks placed), '1788 ... sur les montagnes des Pins à gauche et en montant au Rocher. ... Montagne des Pins à droite en montante au Rocher' (*Arch. Nat.* O¹, 1882). In 1791, every few days during January, February, March of that year, trees were torn up from the montagnes. In April, 1792, 'Journée à arracher les Thujas sur les montagnes' (O¹, 1879).

116

A Rêverie

trickling stream pouring over the rocks at her right hand, amidst ferns and moss, on its way into the grotto below the bridge.

Sitting under the north terrace near the door leading from the house to the Jeu de Bague, she had re-opened and re-read the minister's letter whilst waiting for the carriage. Womanlike, the Queen remembered that the dress she had been wearing that morning was one of the light skirts repaired during that summer, the green silk bodice made in July, a large white fichu, and a straw hat.[1]

At that moment two of the many strangers who now came in as they liked passed her by and even went up on to the terrace behind her by the staircase at her left hand.[2] The Queen knew that her concierge (Bonnefoy Du Plan)[3] was informed that she was there, and would certainly, on seeing them from his attic window over the chapel, send someone to ask them to go further from the house. It might not have been wise, but her old servants had done all they dared to protect her privacy. She had before now, when wandering about alone, heard the coldness and un-concern with which the Bersy brothers had directed strangers in the grounds. Just as she had expected, a moment later, the Queen had heard the slam of the chapel door[4] and had thought that Lagrange[5] would probably conduct them into the avenue by the passage of the *porte de la ménagerie*, that being the nearest way out of the gardens.[6]

The carriage was ready, and the moment had come for rallying her force to act the part of a true queen in whatever circum-

[1] Reiset, pp. 365, 369, 404, 423.
[2] After May, 1789, the grounds were thrown open (Desjardins, p. 345).
[3] Desjardins, pp. 188, 189.
[4] The great door of the chapel, which led into the royal gallery, opened upon a terrace then joined to the western terrace of the house.
[5] The name of the Suisse (in 1789) in charge of the *porte du perron de la Chapelle* was Lagrange. His rooms were behind the chapel (Desjardins, p. 189).
[6] According to M. de Nolhac (see note to *Consignes de Marie Antoinette*, p. 7) the *porte de la ménagerie* should be placed near the buildings of the kitchens and conciergerie. In Mique's map (1783) a broad passage led through these buildings from the French garden to the avenue.

stances were before her. The vivid dream was over, and in proportion as her retrospect was concerned with more important matters, the details stood out less clearly in her mind.

There was no refreshment in going over the events of the rest of that day; though some of them came back to her in rapid succession. The hurried return of the King from hunting at Meudon; the councils; the variations of policy; the presence of a rough and alarming-looking crowd on the Place d'Armes; the free fights; the deputation of women escorted by Mounier on the part of the Assembly; then the final ordering of the carriages too late for escape; the heavy depressing rain from 4 p.m. onwards which at last helped to clear away the crowd; the arrival at midnight of Lafayette and his national guard. All had been confusing and miserable. But agitating as the 5th had been, there was no comparison between it and the tension of October 6th.

The Queen remembered that she had only gone to bed that morning at 2 a.m. in order that her ladies might have some rest, but for herself there was none. Both on October 6th, 1789, and now on August 10th, 1792, outside disturbances had begun at 5 a.m. amidst the glories of a perfect summer dawn. But on the former occasion it had been first realised in one of her own suite of rooms. She had heard the sounds of actual fighting close to her bedroom, and the hasty shout of the guards, 'Sauvez la Reine!' informed her of their deadly peril. The escape to the King's room and the gathering of the family together was quickly effected; but the comfort of the reunion had been followed by terrible hours when Lafayette had done his utmost to quell the fury of the mob. There had been amongst it a company of, as it seemed, veritable fiends, come from no one knew where, whose faces were terrible to look at.[1] It was they who enacted the horrid

[1] 'Parmi eux se trouvoient des hommes de figure étrange, ce qui sembloient y avoir été appelés; car le peuple de Paris a sa physionomie, et ceux qui le connoissent savent bien distinguer les étrangers qui

A Rêverie

scene of beheading the two murdered guards (Varicourt and Deshuttes) under the royal windows in the Cour de Marbre; and until they marched off to Paris carrying with them the two decapitated heads on spikes, it was impossible to come to any terms with the mob. But after their departure, by Lafayette's wish (which at that time amounted to command), first the King and then the Queen had ventured on to the balcony, and had been greeted with some warmth.

And now, three years later, they had not the protecting influence of Lafayette to depend on, nor even the doubtful friendship of Mirabeau. The mob had gained the upper hand, and seemed to be altogether composed of wild beasts thirsting for blood. Who would save them from the horrible crowd pressing against the *grille?* It had not been without relief that Marie Antoinette had just heard the decree passed to keep them in the building where they were for the night. But what afterwards? Clearly they were not to go back to the Tuileries. The mention of the Luxembourg palace was interesting; still more so, the arguments of the opposition that it contained dangerous subterranean passages and opportunities for escape. The Queen's brain was eagerly at work again, and intensely conscious of the present.

But Madame Royale and the Dauphin had borne all they could, and at 7 p.m. Madame de Tourzel was allowed to see the accommodation being prepared for the party in the cells of the ancient

s'y confondent. Ces bandes farouches avoient précédé la garde nationale, dont il faut bien la distinguer; elles causèrent tout le désordre du lendemain. ... Au dehors, les brigands s'étoient emparés de deux gardes du corps; ils leur coupèrent la tête, malgré les efforts de ceux des gardes nationaux qui arrivoient. ... Enfin cette bande de scélérats reprit la route de Paris, emportant en signe de victoire les deux têtes des gardes des corps. Avec eux disparut toute l'horreur des scènes sanglantes du matin. Alors le caractère national se montra dans toute sa candeur. Les soldats parisiens et les gardes du roi s'embrassent.'—M. J. P. Rabaut, *Almanach Historique de la Révolution Française,* pp. 151–153.

This was written in 1791, and Rabaut was guillotined later 'comme Girondin.'

119

couvent des Feuillants. It was not till 10 p.m. that they were escorted thither by representatives of the Assembly; but for the elders it was neither to rest nor to sleep, for they were still within sound of the fierce mob outside as well as of the distant hum of the all-powerful Assembly about to decree their final destiny.

Three more weary days and nights spent in much the same manner were forced upon the unhappy family before they were conducted to the Temple, and into what proved to be for the majority of them the valley of the shadow of death.

E.M.

November,1908

CHAPTER V

Appendix[1]

In September, 1908, I went over again to the Trianon to get some photographs which we wished to have but I found great difficulty in being admitted to the gardener's yard, as leave had to be given at his private door. I did however take a photograph of the inside of the large double gates, but stacks of planks were placed near, as it seemed with the intent of blocking these doors; some of the planking had already been built up into a covering for the inside of the wall. When in the English garden I found the *porte d'entrée* open, and with the gardener's permission took photographs of the inside of the wall in which were both the *porte d'entrée* and the *petite porte*. The latter had evidently been long disused, as the door showed signs of having been already blocked up, but it was being further masked by a wall of planking which would soon entirely conceal it. There was a long, newly built shed in which planking was being prepared. I wrote to Miss Moberly to tell her this, upon which she answered from England and asked me to go over once more if possible to get photographs of the rock staircase and the other places we had visited, lest they too should disappear before we had another chance.

I went at once the next day, September 12th, the only day I had left, and took all the photographs I could. It was a sunshiny windy day and there were plenty of people about, several of

[1] Added in 1924 ed. Bodley MS. Eng. misc. d. 252, fol. 133.

An Adventure

whom stopped me to ask the way. The last photograph I took was that of the cottage roofs, and I turned to go away, glad and relieved to find that there was just time to catch the tram and the train back. As the quickest way out of the grounds I went towards the old *logement du corps de garde*, and as I turned the corner of the old wall I saw two women sitting in the shade, not far from the old gateway, which, in 1901, had been open. They were disputing in loud voices. As I passed the *corps de garde*, suddenly and utterly unexpectedly I knew that some indefinable change had taken place. I felt as though I were being taken up into another condition of things quite as real as the former. The women's voices, though their quarrel was just as shrill and eager as before, seemed to be fading so quickly away that they would soon be altogether gone; from their tones the dispute was clearly still going on, but seemed to have less and less power to reach me.

I turned at once to look back, and saw the gates near which they were sitting melting away, and the background of trees again becoming visible through them as on our original visit, but I noticed that the side pillars were standing steady.[1] The whole scene—sky, trees, and buildings—gave a little shiver, like the movement of a curtain or of scenery as at a theatre. At the same time the old difficulty of walking on and of making any way reproduced itself, together with the feeling of depression described in 1901.

In a moment I decided to keep to my plan of going straight out by the lane, and once outside the lane things became natural again. But the sudden, startling sense of insecurity left a deep impression, so little did I expect any repetition of the old phenomena after the innumerable uneventful visits I had paid to the Trianon since the winter of 1902.

E. F. JOURDAIN

[1] [These pillars were old and probably had not been renewed since their original erection. Added in 1911 ed.]

122

Appendix

II

It was in 1908 (seven years after our first visit to Versailles) that we obtained an ancient map of the grounds of the Petit Trianon by Contant de la Motte in 1783 (Pl. II and III). In it we found the Queen's grotto, the old road through what is now the kitchen buildings, the ancient wood beyond the stream, as well as the old cottage where the woman and girl had been seen, but there was no sign of the little ravine. All these things had been destroyed by Louis Philippe, and were absent therefore from modern maps of the place. In the winter of 1912 we wrote for permission to publish it, and were told in reply that Mique's original manuscript map[1] had been found. A photographed copy of the manuscript map was sent to us, and our French correspondent asked us to notice the slight discrepancies between it and Contant de la Motte' reproduction of it. To our great interest we found in it the indication of the position of the little ravine exactly where we had seen it in 1901.

The following summer (1913) we went to one of the libraries at Versailles and asked to see the actual map and to hear its history. Here we were told that in 1903 it had been rescued from a house in Montmorency, where it had formed part of the stuffing of a chimney. The chimney had been cleared and the crumpled plan, charred by fire and smoke, had been sent to the library, in case it might prove to be valuable. It was considered to be of great value, for Louis XVI had made notes on it in his own handwriting.

Now the year 1903 was two years after we had seen and crossed over the ravine by the little bridge and had described it to many people both by word and writing. Also, it was five years before we had discovered from the gardener's wages-book (the

[1] [In the Archives Départementales at Versailles. It is in fact signed by 'M. Contant de la Motte Ingénieur Géographe 1781' but is doubtless copied from plans by Mique. J.E.]

old fastenings of which had been broken at the national archives in Paris) that there must have been such a ravine in that part of the grounds.

This removed the whole incident of our having passed over it from the possibility of telepathy between living persons, for in 1901 no living person could have seen the manuscript plan; it was in no library and was inaccessible.

C.A.E.M.

E.F.J.

III

On the afternoon of 14th August in the same summer of 1913 we had the pleasure of walking through the grounds of the Petit Trianon with two French gentlemen,[1] the one a distinguished University man, and the other in command of a French regiment and also an examiner for the French army and navy. The colonel said that he had no preconceived opinion about our story, thinking it unreasonable to judge of it on *a priori* grounds; but he had hoped to be able some day to have the opportunity of asking us questions and to make up his mind in the place.

We followed the route taken by us in 1901, as far as the modern changes allowed, and we pointed out the differences made in the gardens that had taken place between our first and second visits. Standing at the exact spot where we had spoken to the guards, the colonel questioned us closely about the shape, colour, and every detail of their uniforms. He said that greyish-green would have been an unusual colour in the French army in 1789, but that if the men we saw were stationed in a place like Trianon as *gardes des portes*, or *gardes des bosquets*, or *gardes forestiers*, they would have worn that colour, and that our detailed description of the uniforms was perfectly correct. We told

[1] [M. Fannière and Colonel Malagutti. J.E.]

him that we had since discovered that the comte d'Artois had been, in 1789, *colonel général des gardes Suisses,* and that his livery was green, but we did not know whether that was to the point. The answer was yes, certainly, the *gardes des portes* formed part of the *gardes Suisses,* and everyone under the command of the comte d'Artois would have worn his livery and not the King's. The colonel added that we could not possibly have known a point like this unless we had actually seen the men, for none of the details we mentioned were matters of general information, and for us would have required extensive research. This, he said, he could vouch for, because, having written a book about former French uniforms, he was an authority on the subject and knew how difficult—if not impossible—it would have been for us to have obtained the information.

After pointing out the positions of the ravine and pretty little bridge, the tiny cascade, and the kiosk, and noticing the difference of levels and of the general appearance between the present condition and what we had previously seen, the two gentlemen went over the ground and satisfied themselves that the present paths had been dug out of what might have been the side of a hill. They looked at the iron grids in the pathway, which suggested that water had once come from higher ground. They agreed that if the 'kiosk' had once stood where we had seen it, and was identical with the 'ruine', it might have formed the *naissance de la rivière.* They also inspected the base of a column now hidden in a bush, probably in its wrong place, and thus reconstructed, as far as possible, the ancient aspect of that part of the English garden.

We then went to the terrace still remaining round the north and west sides of the house and showed our companions where we had seen the ancient terrace which joined the chapel to the house, passing along one side of the chapel courtyard. The colonel was surprised and inclined to doubt it, for he said the present effect was 'bien symétrique', and that was what Frenchmen prized. But after making his own investigations he owned that he could see that the wall of the chapel courtyard had been altered, and that there might have been a terrace at the level of the chapel steps. He enquired about the dress of 'the man from the chapel', suggesting that it might have been that of an abbé, but he assented to our objection that an abbé would not have appeared without his cassock. He also agreed that, even if we had imaginatively clothed real people with eighteenth-century dresses (this had been suggested to us), no imagination on our part could have succeeded in altering the scenery to what it had been a hundred years before.

It was wonderfully interesting. We were in some ways the hosts, for the invitation to the expedition had been ours, and we were describing from memory the exact position of points in some ancient scenery of more than a hundred years before; but our guests were the Frenchmen, whose national possession it was, and whose personal interest in its associations was, we soon found out, greater than ours. Then we were not being asked for *impossible explanations*, but questions were being put to us, leading to instant examination into the facts by people who were authorities about the details of the history and accustomed to deal with the configuration of the ground and local maps. When we had stated at each place exactly what we had seen, they supplied us in return with the explanation. For instance, when we pointed out the house which had contained the carved staircase, they told us the reasons why such a house would almost certainly have had one when it was first built, and why it had now been taken away; and this they inferred from the type of building before them.

At the end of the expedition, the colonel said that at first such a story as ours had seemed incredible to him, but that now he had had the opportunity of acting as the *avocat du diable* and of putting forward every objection that had occurred to him; and having heard our answers to his questions asked on the spot, he was not only satisfied with our good faith, but was ready to accept the story as it stood.

After reading this account of our walk, one of the French gentlemen countersigned it, adding the words, 'I can testify to the accuracy of every detail in the said account.'

[Appendix IV of the 1924 edition has been omitted as it concerns experiences of people other than Miss Moberly and Miss Jourdain.]

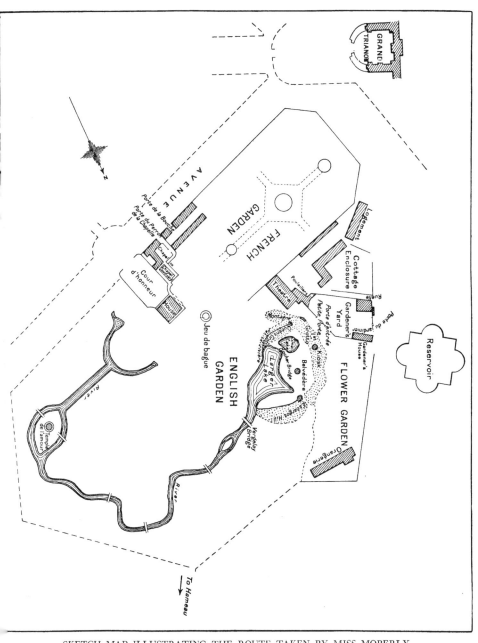

GRAND TRIANON

N

AVENUE

Porte de la Bouche
Porte du Parc
Porte de la Chapelle

FRENCH GARDEN

Cour d'honneur

Jeu de bague

ENGLISH GARDEN

River

Temple de l'amour

Cottage
Logement

Enclosure

Gardener's Yard

Pont-Neuf

Porte d'entrée
Petite Porte

Montagne

Grotto
Kiosk

Belvédère

Garden Lake

Belvédère Hill

Varéglay Bridge

Gardener's House

Porte du jardinier

Ruelle

FLOWER GARDEN

Orangerie

Reservoir

River

To Hameau

SKETCH MAP ILLUSTRATING THE ROUTE TAKEN BY MISS MOBERLY
AND MISS JOURDAIN ON THE 10TH AUGUST 1901

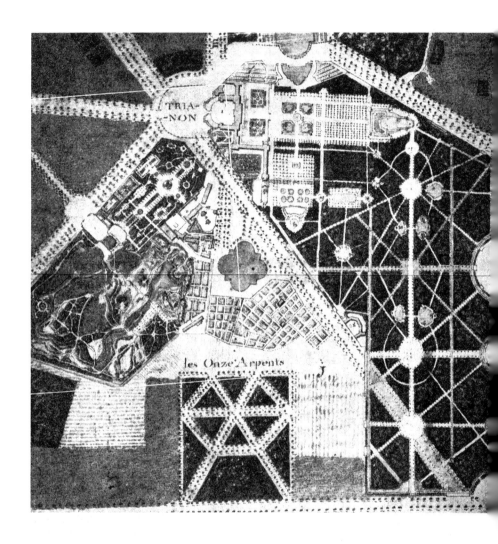

MIQUE'S MAP OF THE GARDENS OF THE TRIANON

ENLARGED SECTION OF MIQUE'S MAP
(an enlargement of the area within white square on Plate II)

VERSAILLES AND THE TRIANONS IN 1898
From a plan made by Marcel Lambert

Index

Index

Index